PRACTICAL APPLICATION OF CLASSROOM MANAGEMENT THEORIES INTO STRATEGIES

Edited by
George R. Taylor

University Press of America,® Inc.
Dallas · Lanham · Boulder · New York · Oxford

Copyright © 2004 by
University Press of America,® Inc.
4501 Forbes Boulevard
Suite 200
Lanham, Maryland 20706
UPA Acquisitions Department (301) 459-3366

PO Box 317
Oxford
OX2 9RU, UK

Library of Congress Control Number: 2003111861
ISBN 0-7618-2730-7 (paperback : alk. ppr.)

Dedication

This book is dedicated to personnel in the public and private sector serving children with disabilities.

Contents

List of Figures and Tables

Preface

A knowledge of classroom management strategies are essential for teachers when dealing with inappropriate and unacceptable behaviors in the classroom. This is especially true for prospective teachers. The need to: (1) Have a knowledge of how to manage classrooms with children from diverse environments, and (2) A knowledge of how to employ strategies based upon the behavior problems being presented; and how to effectively diagnose behavior problems.

Recent federal laws involving inclusion of individuals with disabilities have added to the mounting behavior problems that both pre and in-service teachers face. Teachers need specific skills in : (1) Classroom management strategies, Including instruction in responding to chronic behavior problems, (2) Using human and physical resources at school and the community to reduce maladaptive behavior, (3) Involving parents in developing discipline plans, and (4) Evaluating the effectiveness of the discipline plan.

This text is designed to accomplish the above strategies by enabling teachers to create conducive classrooms where students feel empowered rather than unempowered. Each chapter in the text is designed to assist teachers in developing a positive and creative classroom environment.

Acknowledgments

Classroom management strategies discussed in this text have been developed over a period of 25 years. They were developed while observing students in practica settings. We readily recognized that classroom management strategies were necessary for students to implement if they were to have an effective instructional program. As a result, this text was written to address this critical need. Specific strategies have been outlined to assist both pre and in-service teachers in implementing effective classroom management strategies.

We recognize that this text would not have been developed without the assistance of others. The staff at Rosemont Elementary School provided the opportunity for us to observe pre and in-service teachers in the classroom. We are also appreciative to Mrs. Karen Chewing and Mrs. Emma Crosby for typing the manuscript, and to Dr. Marcellina Brooks for editing the manuscript, and the staff a Scarecrow Press for their invaluable assistance in preparing the final manuscript.

Chapter 1

Causes Associated with Classroom Management and Discipline Problems

George R Taylor

Overview

Classroom problems have their genesis early in the lives of children. Problems such as poor or impoverished environments, diverse backgrounds, placement in   inclusive classrooms and parental management styles have all contributed to class room management and discipline problems. These societal problems are not solely responsible for classroom problems in the schools. The schools must also assume some of the behavioral problems. School related problems contributing to discipline problem may include poor curricula and instructional planning, poor learning environment, not addressing the needs of children, poor parental involvement, lack of understanding principles of child development and not having a well defined discipline program. These and more issues containing discipline and classroom management techniques will be addressed in Chapters 10 and 11, all designed to asset educators in understanding some of the problems associated with discipline and classroom problems.

Early Environment Experiences

Children born in poverty and neglect often suffer from debilitating deprivation that seriously impairs their abilities to learn. Early prevention programs for these children and their parents (starting with prenatal care and including health care, quality day care, and preschool education) help prevent learning that disrupts later educational efforts

(Butler, 1989). A key reason that some individuals have such a high rate of educational failure and discipline problems is that they often lag in physical and psychological development and may be unprepared to meet the demands of academic learning. There is evidence to support that the lack of early experiences can affect brain development. Some areas of the brain require adequate stimulation at the right time in order to take on their normal functions (Steinberg, 1996). From case studies of some individuals, findings indicate that there may be critical periods for cognitive and language development (Hatch and Gardner, 1988).

Intervention in the early years appears to be the most effective way to improve the prospects for individuals to receive maximum benefits from their educational experiences. Impoverishment of a child's early environmental experiences including any major restrictions on play activities or lack of feedback from older individuals, is suspected or retarding his/her social development and learning. Lack of adequate adult stimulation in the early years can lead to individuals developing negative social behavior which may be irreversible. First, in the absence of adequate stimulation and activity, neurophysiological mechanisms involved in learning may fail to develop. Second, conditions, impoverished environments, such as the slums, generally do not provide variety of duration of exposure to perceptual-motor experiences compared to children from affluent environments (Dalli, 1991; Dewitt, 1994; Ayers, 1989).

Children learn violent behaviors early. By the time they are in high school, they are lost. Educators need to start with the three year olds and teach them more appropriate ways to handle frustration, such as thinking about the consequences of their behaviors and decisions (Taylor, 1998).

Children in mismatched environments often leave the environment or become less productive in it. Individuals are influenced by elements within their environments. An individual who lives in an environment that is a good match for his needs and abilities will likely be more productive and tend to reflect the character of that environment. Children in mismatched environments often have trouble transferring values from one environment to another; therefore, many leave school when they reach the legal age. Individuals do a great deal of learning outside of the classroom. They have accomplished a vast amount of nonacademic learning before they enter school, and continue to learn nonacademic sources while they are enrolled. Many of these learning experiences are in conflict with standards imposed by the school, thus creating behavior problems in the classroom. Values, styles, and concepts that individuals bring to the schools must be matched and integrated into their own social reality if school experiences are to be meaningful.

Research reported by Erikson as early as 1959 supported that environments characterized by mistrust, doubt, limitations, feelings of inferiority and powerlessness are factors that contribute to identify confusion and inhibit the development of the mature individual (Erikson, 1959). In support of Erikson's view, Ayers (1989) wrote that children need the home base of family life in order to grow up healthy and strong. They need to be listened to and understood, nurtured and challenged by caring, committed adults. Parents need to contribute to their childrens' self-esteem, self-activity or self-control through appropriate modeling strategies.

If a child's early development status and early home environment are dysfunctional, there is an increased likelihood of poor developmental outcomes. The home environment should be where the child receives support, experiences, love, and acquires important skills in becoming a productive, happy, social, and emotional person. The home environment is the foundation for further development within the child. Experiences from the home should be integrated with the school curriculum for meaningful experiences to occur, which will necessitate, including the family and the community in the education process (Kagan, 1989).

Impoverish Background

Children from impoverished backgrounds have different needs and characteristics than their peers from other environments. Teachers need to understand these needs and characteristics in designing classroom management strategies. According to (Payne, 1998) the following behaviors are related to children from impoverished backgrounds:

1. Laughs when disciplined; is disrespectful to the teacher;
2. Argues loudly with the teacher;
3. Responds angrily;
4. Uses inappropriate or vulgar comments;
5. Fights to survive or uses verbal abuse with other students;
6. Hands are always on someone else;
7. Can't follow directions;
8. Is extremely disorganized;
9. Talks incessantly;
10. Cheats or steals.

Cummings (2000) estimated that 25% of school age children may exhibit the above behaviors.

Children from Diverse Backgrounds

Children from diverse backgrounds have increased the need for improvement in classroom management techniques (Cummings, 2000). Research by Fuchs, Fuchs, Mathes, and Simmons, (1997) revealed that 26% of children in this country had limited English proficiency and that 24% were immigrants. Data from the National Center for Educational Statistics (1999) stated that less than half of U.S. teachers feel sufficiently trained to react to the needs of children from diverse backgrounds. Teachers need to be better trained to make modifications in their instructional programs that provide more realistic conditions attuned to their environments and learning styles. When the aforementioned is not sufficiently addressed, patterns of resistance and oppositions are commonly reactions. These reactions frequently manifest themselves in breaking school rules and presenting behavior problems in the classroom (Ogbu, 1988).

Specials Populations

Disabilities of individuals may interfere with their abilities to remain on-task and complete assigned activities. Accommodations may need to be made to assist many of these students. Students with disabilities may be characterized as having physical, communication, intellectual or social emotional disorders. Impairments in these areas may range from mild to severe. Each type of disability is unique and may constitute specialized classroom management techniques and strategies. The types of characteristics and complexities of special populations are too involved to be adequately covered in this section. The reader is referred to the listed source.*

Federal mandates and regulations, as well as local and state regulations, and ruling from litigations provide a wide array of legal issues to consider in using classroom management strategies with children with disabilities. Many of the federal regulations are found in the federal statues known as "IDEA" (Hallahan & Kauffman, 1997; Turnbull & Turnbull, 1998). Two major components of IDEA that teachers and educators should be acutely aware of are: 1) Zero Reject, and 2) development of the Individualized Education Plan (IEP). Zero-reject implications have many ramifications for classroom management. The

---

*George R. Taylor (2001) Educational Intervention and Services for Children with Exceptionalities: Strategies and Perspectives, Springfield, IL: Charles C. Thomas

Supreme Court has made many decisions relevant to expulsion of individuals with disabilities, some of the findings according to Turnbull & Turnbull (1998) includes:

1. That if students behaviors are connected to manifestation of their disabilities, expulsion would violate IDEA rule of Zero Reject.
2. Local education agencies (LEA) may not discipline a student if the behavior that triggered the discipline was a manifestation of the student's disability.
3. That a student whose behavior is a manifestation of a disability may be disciplined, but significant limitations are placed on the discipline procedures and on the type of discipline which may be imposed.

These summaries of court rulings pinpoint the importance of educators being fully aware of the laws under Individuals with Disabilities Educations Act (IDEA). Concerning legal responsibilities, teachers and educators should contact the Director of Special Education or a person charged with administering special education programs.

Individualized education program (IEP) is also mandated by IDEA. An IEP should specify the resources, services, support, and authority required to deliver instructional services. It is developed for each special education student by the IEP team members. The team include the parents, at least or regular teacher, at least a special education teacher, a representative from the school district who is qualified to meet the needs of students, and other individuals deemed appropriate by the team. An IEP is a written agreement between the parents and the school district that specifies an assessment of the student, the services to be provided, instructional plans and evaluation of services. These approaches have significant implications for how teachers can employ classroom management strategies and techniques.

Inclusive Classrooms

Due to federal legislations, P.L. 94 – 142 and IDEA, a significant number of children with disabilities are being educated in regular classrooms. Many children with disabilities have physical and other problems which may interfere with their social interactions in the classroom (Taylor, 1998). Teachers need to be aware of these problems and plan instruction accordingly. Many children with disabilities have learned destructive ways of demonstrating inappropriate behaviors in the classroom, chiefly because they have not been taught appropriate ways of dealing with their behaviors. Specific strategies must be developed to assist these children in internalizing their behaviors. Many of the strategies to improve classroom behaviors discussed in Chapters 3 – 9 can be modified and adapted for children with disabilities. It is essential that teachers have the use of supportive services, if needed, to develop and maintain appropriate classroom management techniques to aid children with disabilities in self correcting or maintaining appropriate behaviors.

Parental Management Styles

Steinberg (1996) wrote that parenting styles can affect a child's success in school. He further stated that the authoritative parent is much more successful than the permissive parent. On the other hand, the permissive parent does not set clear goals for the child. The authoritative parent draws from both approaches by setting clear limits, providing guidance, setting high standards, encouraging independence, and valuing input from children.

Parents employ a variety of techniques for controlling and shaping the behaviors of their children. Parents who are abusive can directly attribute to their children's behavior problems. Parents who are aggressive mean to control behaviors of their children may influence aggressive behaviors of their children or others. Parents should be a role model for their children, and demonstrate behaviors that they wish their children to emulate. If parents do not provide guidance by personal examples of their major values, it is almost impossible to assist children in emulating desired behaviors (Cullingford, 1996). Teachers and educators must realize that many behaviors demonstrated in the classroom, negative and positive, are a direct manifestation of parental styles and behavior strategies enforced or practiced at home (Taylor, 2000).

The Role of the School

Studies have consistently shown that negative behaviors are learned behaviors which children imitate from their environments. These behaviors manifest themselves in hostile and destructive patterns of behavior, which frequently cannot be controlled by the schools, thus creating conflict and tension between children, parents, and school (Matseuda & Heimer, 1987; Taylor, 1992).

The preponderance of studies in the area of social learning, have consistently shown that the learning styles of children must be programmed into the instructional program (Biehler & Snowman, 1982). The school have failed to capitalize on this salient point. The school has not changed its basic approach to teaching over the last several decades. In spite of the vast amount of research and literature on innovative teaching techniques and strategies, school experiences for many children are usually unrelated to the experiences they bring to school. Their abilities to function satisfactorily in social groups are usually below expected levels set by the school. They have fewer and less rigid control over their impulses and have learned hostile and destructive patterns of behavior as viewed by society and the school. Many children will never become fully integrated in society and the school unless early intervention is attempted and social and behavioral skills are infused and systematically taught throughout the curriculum. It is incumbent upon the school to recognize and accept this fact and to develop strategies to modify, adapt, and gradually promote what is considered to be "appropriate behavior" through the use of behavior intervention techniques and other strategies.

The impact of personality temperament, cognitive styles, sociological influences, and ethnic background may all influence development of social skills needed to successfully control and monitor one's behavior in the classroom (Taylor, 1998). The study of social learning theories enables the school to both understand how these children's cultures can be modified to promote expected learning outcomes as well as how they feel about themselves in relationship to learning.

Early intervention services should include strategies to promote physical, mental, social and emotional, language and speech, and management skills The key is early intervention, which should be designed to treat, prevent and reduce environmental factors associated with the impediment of social growth and development. Research findings listed above indicated that teachers and educators must be aware of factors associated with discipline problems. Lack of this understanding may contribute to behavior problems in the classroom.

Transforming the Environment

A major factor affecting how well a child functions in his environment is self-esteem. Promoting self-esteem among children assists in reducing behavior problems which will surface later in life. Additional research is needed in this area to evaluate the impact of strategies and programs designed to promote self-esteem.

Educational leaders need empirical data on the effectiveness of programs to raise self-esteem of children. High self-esteem appears to promote confidence, security, citizenship, and academic success. Some recommended strategies or principles for improving self-concepts and behaviors of children are as follows:

1.   Praise rather than criticize.
2.   Teach children to set achievable goals.
3.   Teach children to praise themselves and to capitalize on their strong points.

4.   Teach children to praise others.
5.   Set realistic expectation levels.
6.   Teach children to have confidence in themselves.
7.   Praise children for achieving or failing after attempting to achieve.
8.   Praise children for successfully completing a test or project.
9.   Praise children for positive criticism.
10.   Accept pupils contribution without judgment.
11.   Listen to children, they have important information to share.
12.   Maintain a "you can do it" philosophy.
13.   Present challenges for children.
14.   Provide movement and freedom within the classroom for children to achieve objectives.
15.   Show concern and warmth.
16.   Set high classroom control strategies with input from children.
17.   Demonstrate and show respect for children.
18.   Provide an atmosphere for success.
19.   Listen to how you talk to children.
20.   Catch someone doing something right and tell him/her about it.
21.   Attack the behavior, not the student, separate the behavior from the child.
22.   Use modeling or other techniques to reduce maladaptive behavior.
23.   Teach children to respect themselves and others.
24.   Teach children to be proud of their heritage.
25.   Provide activities which incorporate parental involvement.

These strategies are not inconclusive and should be expanded as assessed by the teachers (Taylor, 1998).

Standards to Maintain Discipline

Teachers who develop standards and expectations with children, and model ways for achieving them, have lower discipline problems. This approach to classroom management is frequently called proactive. We have addressed the issue in greater detail in Chapter 11. Teachers who are proactive teach self control by means of developing a pre set list of standards and expectations for children to follow (Charney, 1992). Children should have a direct part in developing the standards and the expectations. These standards and expectations should be frequently reviewed and modified when needed. Parents should be apprised of the standards and expectations and their environment should be sought (Taylor, 2000).

Factors in the Society

Due to various factors within society and the community, the schools' role in enhancing self-esteem is of prime importance. Intervention must be made early to break or prevent failure due to low self-esteem. There appears to be a positive relationship between reduced discipline problems, self-concept and student's success or failure in school (Taylor, 1992).

There are many factors influencing children's development prior to going to school. When the school accepts the child, it should be committed to accepting and attempting to teach the "whole child," not just developing the three R's. A major factor in a child's development in the beginning school years in the child's view of himself/herself as he/she communicates with other students. Individuals as well as other students' self-concept influences their motivation to learn and behave appropriately. If students do not feel good about themselves generally, and good about themselves specifically as learners, they will lack the motivation to improve their behavioral performances in the classroom. Group and individual activities are needed in order to improve the self-concepts. Specific activities have been developed to improve self-concept in Chapters 3 – 9.

The role of the teacher in promoting self-control of children cannot be over-emphasized. The teacher exerts considerable influence on shaping a child's self-concept through the type of treatments, beliefs and expectations imposed upon the child. Children quickly react to and easily interpret negative traits projected by the teacher. The child's interpretation of the teacher's actions and their significance play an important role in how the child reacts.

Children sift, seek, reject, and avoid information from individuals they do not respect or trust. They do not accept information from adults who have rejected them as readily but they do from adults who they feel have accepted them and are trustworthy. Rejection at home or at school may promote children to seek elsewhere for acceptance, such as gangs or peer pressures. Gangs and peer pressures may contribute significantly to shaping a student's behavior.

Teachers can exert significant influence on the forming of the child's self-concept by the constructive and positive learning environments as well as showing positive attitudes and developing rapport toward children (Taylor, 1998).

A Holistic Approach

Children are being educated in substandard schools in some school districts. We have not done a satisfactory job in providing quality education for these individuals. The schools have failed in educating the "whole child." According to a recent report by the National Association of State Boards of Education (1992), it was voiced that a holistic view that is attuned to the students' nonacademic needs must be included as part of his/her instructional program, which includes social, emotional, personal and citizenship training.

Instruction that minimizes the teaching of social and civic responsibility in the quest for academic excellence may not produce well informed citizens in our society. Findings by other researchers have voiced similar concerns (Biklen, 1989; Forest, 1990; Barth, 1990; Eisner, 1991; O'Brien & O'Brien, 1991; Ogbu, 1988). They also support a holistic integrated approach to educating children. It was recommended that to avoid fragmenting school experiences, students' social and emotional well-being must be integrated and infused into a total program emphasizing social and interpersonal needs, communication needs, and academic needs. The schools must begin to use the vast amount of research present to experiment with various ways of including social skills development into the curriculum if disabled individuals are to achieve up to their maximum potentials.

The concept of teaching the "whole child" has been advocated since the beginning of this century. Historically, the school has mainly focused on academics, not the emotional development of children. To minimize the number of discipline problems in the classroom all of the aforementioned factors must be considered by the teacher, in order to make teaching and learning functional and meaningful to children.

The educational application of emotional research is still in its infancy. Some general principles to guide classroom applications are:

1.   Seek to develop forms of self-control among students and staff that encourages nonjudgemental, nondisruptive venting of emotions.
2.   Schools should focus more on metacognitive activities that encourage students to talk about their emotions, listen to their classmates' feelings.
3.   Activities that emphasize social interaction and that engage the entire body tend to provide the most emotional support.

4.   School activities that draw out emotions-stimulations, role playing, and cooperative projects may provide important contextual memory prompts.

5.   Emotionally stressful school environments are counterproductive because they can reduce a students' ability to learn (Brigge & Hunt, 1968).

Over time, children tend to develop habitual ways of responding to experiences. Children are a product of their environment. The importance of emotions in teaching children, attention, learning and memory, are all associated with one's emotions. This concept does not appear to be readily understood by educators, thus it is not adequately reflected in the curriculum. The school should conduct empirical studies showing the relationship between an emotionally positive classroom and the academic achievement, and the emotional health of pupils (Kandel & Kandel, 1994; Vincent, 1990).

Our emotional system is a complex, widely distributed and error-prone system that defines our basic personality early in life, and is quite resistant to change. The clear implication of this research is that positive models and early interventions are needed if healthy emotions are to emerge. The emotional system is a complex process under the direction and supervision of the brain. It is frequently viewed as a more powerful determinant of our behavior that our rational processes. A detailed discussion of the emotional system is outside the scope of this text. Please refer to Chapter endnotes for additional sources.

Cummins (1984) findings supported educating the "whole child." He assessed traditional instruction models currently used by the public schools to educate children. These models are mostly based upon cognitive theories and include: 1) analysis of academic tasks, 2) the establishment of sequential learning objectives based on each task analysis, and 3) direct instruction of individual task components. Most instruction and teaching in the public schools are based on the aforementioned models (Tharp, 1989; Poplin, 1988). Many children have various learning styles and frequently cannot achieve success with these traditional models. Strategies and interventions must focus on the individual needs of children. The approach must be integrated and coordinated with available community resources.

Many children may have developed or adapted alternative ways and styles of coping with problems in their neighborhoods. These behavioral styles are frequently in conflict with the school and society in general and may be viewed as negative or destructive. Behavioral styles and models copied and imitated by children may serve them well in their environments, but are frequently viewed as dysfunctional by the school and society.

As indicated throughout this book, instructional program must be developed and designed to enable children to gain knowledge about appropriate interpersonal skills, and to employ this newly-acquired knowledge in solving their social problems. In order for this goal to be accomplished, children must be taught effective ways of internalizing their behaviors, and assessing how their behaviors affect others. Teaching appropriate social skills to children in the classroom appears to be promising techniques for improving behavior and pro-social skills (Taylor, 1992). Appropriate social skills are essential for developing personal relationships and accepting the roles of authority figures. Social behaviors are learned, therefore, they can be changed and modified. They require that an individual evaluate a situation, choose the appropriate social skills, and perform the social tasks appropriately (Katz, 1991). Unfortunately, many children have not been exposed to appropriate social models or do not possess enough prerequisite skills, such as maturity and self-control to successfully perform the social skills.

Summary

Understanding needed by teachers to improve discipline in the classroom. Some children:

1.   Seem generally unaware of the "ground rules" for success in school;
2.   Are less able to learn from being told than are their counterparts;
3.   Are often unable to make simple symbolic interpretations;
4.   Tend to have shorter attention spans, consequently have problems in following directions;
5.   Are unable to use language in a flexible way;
6.   Tend to have little concept of relative size of objects outside of their environments;
7.   Are less likely to perceive adults as people to whom they can turn to for help;
8.   Seem to have a low level of curiosity about things;
9.   Seem to project a low self-image;
10.   Have experiences within a very narrow range.

The difficult part of teaching is not developing appropriate learning strategies for children, but dealing with the great influx of individuals who come from emotionally, physically, socially and financially stressed homes. This is not a school problem alone. Society in general must assume the major responsibilities for these environmental atrocities. School experiences for many children have virtually remained unchanged; are usually unrelated to the experiences they bring to school; and do not adequately address the aforementioned observations outline. Life in school is mostly teacher-centered, textbook-dominated, restrictive, impersonal and rigid (Goodlad, 1984).

These issues and more must be addressed by the school if it is to become responsive to the educational needs of all children. Policies must be changed at the local, state, and national levels. The position advanced by the Committee for Economic Development (1987) stated that, "for imperative and more practical reasons, our commitment to the young must go beyond political rhetoric; it must produce a well-planned curriculum of programs for children from birth through adulthood." This statement implies that a total integrated approach is needed to properly instruct children.

Chapter 2

Classroom Management Theories

Lois Nixon

Overview

An understanding of classroom management theories will provide teachers and other related school personnel with various psychological theories needed to effective control behaviors in the classroom. A knowledge or these theories will enable teachers and related school personnel with an understanding appropriate disciplinary procedures, their own beliefs concerning discipline, and how to infuse their beliefs with student input into an effective classroom discipline program. One of the major groups of theories fall under child development and are usually categorized as management, non-directed or leadership theories. Refer to Chapters 3 – 10.

Management Theories

The philosophy underpinning these theories are based upon developmental and growth principles in which children have little control. Behaviors can be controlled and manipulated through a system of reinforcement and rewards, or by arranging the environment to induce the desired behavior (Kohn, 1993). These theories are based upon principles of behaviorism chiefly advocated by B.F. Skinner and have received wide acceptance. Teachers who endorse this notion that children's behaviors must be controlled, since they are not capable of controlling their own behavior (Martin & Pears, 1992; Taylor, 1998). According to these theories, the ability of the teacher to maintain a safe and effective instructional environment in the classroom requires command of techniques of behavior management (Refer to Chapter 6 for additional details).

Non-Directive Intervention Theories

Edwards (1997) assumptions involving non-directive intervention theories are premised upon the principle that children develop from an inner unfolding. The process may be associated with the innate responses of the child to self correct his/her behaviors. Intervention in the form of external control is not necessary to control behaviors. Children are self-motivated to conform their behaviors to any standard imposed.

Non-directive intervention necessitates a classroom atmosphere and instructional strategies which will encourage self growth. In many instances, the teacher will have to model appropriate behaviors so that children will know how to emulate them. In defense of this theory, (Kerr & Nelson, 1998); Rogers, 1969) supported that children should have considerable freedom in the classroom to direct their own school experiences and that teachers should not fear that children will make inappropriate choices. This approach is similar to strategies advocated in the Ginoft Model, Chapter 4 Glasser Model, Chapter 5, and the Dreikurs Model, Chapter 8. Refer to these models for additional details.

Glasser (1984) is one of the principal advocates of this theory, in which the role of the teacher is essential. Teachers can provide valuable assistance to children as they experiment with various ways to control their behaviors. Modeling accepted behaviors by teachers appear to be an important factor in providing appropriate social experiences for children to demonstrate. Additionally, this theory purports that children want to control their behaviors and can achieve this goal if teachers and responsible adults instruct them how. First, children must internalize their behaviors and recognize, by weighing the negative and positive consequences of their behaviors. The teacher's role is one of leadership and he/she should provide strategies to promote self-directed behaviors for children (Barth, 1990; Rizzo & Zable, 1988).

Leadership Theories

There are many learning theories, however, for the sake of discussion we have grouped them under two broad categories, behavioral and cognitive. These theories assist us in identifying how different individuals may manage, delay, progress through, or retreat from developmental tasks. They also suggest that there are persistent individuals differences such as cognitive and behavioral styles, temperament, or ethnic background that interact with development. Additionally, these theories provide knowledge about individual types and styles that may be critical to our understanding of different sources of reward and punishment for students (Stuart, 1989; Walker, 1995).

Behavioral Theories

Behaviorists believe that students are conditioned by their environments with no innate will to be self-determined, thus human behavior needs to be regulated and controlled through rewards and reinforcement. Self-management is not a goal of behaviorism. (see Chapter 6 for details). Research has shown that cytrinsic reinforcers can significantly undermine intrinsic motivation (Kohn, 1996). Both the negative and positive effects of rewards and reinforcement must be taken in consideration when using behaviorism in controlling behavior. Behavioral techniques may provide the teacher with strategies for assisting children in performing desirable appropriate behaviors. The major purpose is to modify behaviors through rewards and reinforcement. The technique must be systematically employed, the environment constraints must be considered, and teachers and educators using the techniques must be well versed in its use (Taylor, 1998). Principles of behavioral theories may be found in the Jones Model, Chapter 9. Assertive Discipline, Chapter 7 and, Behavior Modification, Chapter 6.

We have attempted to articulate through this text that there are no completed cognitive or behavioral theories reflected in the various management plans. Our view is that effective teachers draw from both broad theoretical perspectives to develop an individualized plan to meet the needs of their individual classes.

Cognitive Theories

Advocates of cognitive theories support the notion and importance of self-regulation. Children are not molded by their environments. The environment may influence behaviors of some children, but children internalize conditions and make decisions on how they behave. This theory supports the premise that children are to be self-directed and to regulate their own behaviors. These theories do not separate the parts from the whole; instead they have a major underlying concept the holistic and interactive nature of development. For example, the various areas of the self do not exist or develop separately from one another, and movement toward maturity in one area can affect movement and learning in another area (Taylor, 1997; Savage, 1991).

Cognitive theories focus on having children to think and internalize their feelings and behaviors before reacting. These strategies are designed to increase self-control of behavior through self-monitoring, self-evaluation and self-reinforcement. Additionally, they are constructed to assist children to compare their behaviors against predetermined standards, and to provide positive and negative feedback to them in order for them to choose and approach (Rizzo & Zabel, 1988). The Druikurs,

Chapter 8, the Gordon Model, Chapter 9, the Ginott Model, Chapter 4, the Kounin Model, Chapter 3, the Glasser Model, Chapter, 5 all draw heavily upon theoretical constructs found in cognitive theories of learning. Refer to the above models and Chapters to identify common threads of cognitive theories embedded in them.

Developing a Model of Discipline

An effective model of discipline for a teacher to employ in a classroom should be developed around his/her beliefs and educational principles. These beliefs and principles usually underpin all activities conducted in and outside of the classroom (Macht, 1990). Edwards, 1997 wrote that without a consistent, well-understood system of beliefs and associated theories, teachers have little guidance in dealing with the complexities of behaviors in the classroom. A teacher may combine and use several discipline theories outlined in the text and formulate his/her own theory based upon the unique needs and characteristics of the class.

One of the first things a teacher should consider before developing a discipline model for classroom management is to be aware of stages and principles of childhood development, management and learning theories and choose from these strategies for developing a model. A basic knowledge of these principles and theories will have a direct bearing on what techniques and strategies teachers will use to promote positive behavior in the classroom. A second requirement that teachers should satisfy before developing a discipline theory, is a basic knowledge of the major discipline theories in use. An effective discipline plan must include all stakeholders in its implementation.

Classroom Discipline Plan

A large percentage of behavioral problems may be prevented by a classroom or discipline plan which is implemented and supported by staff members, administrators, and family members (MacNaughton & Jones, 1991). Consistent classroom behavioral expectations for various activities and settings need to be established and taught. These expectations should reflect the class mission statement and discipline philosophy. The classroom Discipline Plan should include the following elements:

- Classroom discipline philosophy
- Classroom rules
- Common area routines
- Plan for teaching rules and procedures
- System for recognizing expected behaviors
- Description of consistent consequences for infractions

- Emergency procedures to obtain immediate in-school assistance
- System for communication
- Plan for training

Most students will follow the plan and respond with improved behavior.

Strategic Supports for Students

Effective strategic support and structures are needed for those students who display challenging behaviors resulting from unmet needs. A collaborative team approach is helpful in identifying antecedent strategies such as:

- Instructional modifications
- Schedule changes
- Environment changes
- Alternative skills training
- Consequence strategies
- Long-term prevention strategies

Strategic supports and structures are provided; however some of the students will break rules on a regular basis and will require strategic supports and structures for meaningful change (Colvin, Suagi, & Patching, 1998; Walker, Colvin & Ramsey, 1995; Kohn, 1996).

Individualized Student Plans

Despite a classroom discipline plan and positive strategic supports, a small percentage of the students within a classroom will require a personalized student plan to describe an individual program of intervention. A problem-solving process which includes the following elements is helpful in developing the plan:

Identify the behavior
Assess the behavior
Develop hypothesis statements
Select intervention strategies and modifications
Write a plan
Implement the personalized student plan
Document progress
Evaluate the effectiveness of the plan
Modify or terminate the plan

The plan may include:

Background information
Description of the problem and statement of current performance
Goal statements for performance
Hypotheses statements for the function of the behavior

Intervention strategies related to the function of the behavior
Specific evaluation procedures
Supports needed for implementers
Strategies for developing a classroom discipline plan may provide the impetus for developing a school wide discipline plan. Teacher, administrators, parents and students must be committed to the plan and have direct input to its development (Taylor, 2000). Essential to the success of a school wide discipline will be the identification and recognition of the consequences of ones behavior by children. Children may need to have some of the consequences of their behavior model in order for them to fully instance the consequences of their behavior (Kameenui & Simmons, 1990, Kameenui & Darch, 1995).

Challenging Behaviors Serve a Function for the Student

Although problem behaviors may be socially inappropriate, they are driven by the belief that they will produce a desired result for the student (Kauffman, Mostert, Trent, & Hallahan, 1998).
Examples:
Obtaining attention
Escaping/avoiding a task or demand
Obtaining a desired object or activity
Satisfying sensory needs
Gaining control
This belief can be driven by several factors, including past history, observation of others, and a limited repertoire of alternative behaviors. The ultimate goal of student behavior is to fulfill the need to belong by feeling capable, connected, and contributing.

Challenging Behaviors are Context Related

Behaviors do not occur in a vacuum, individuals select (either consciously or unconsciously) behavior in response to their environment. There exist several types of environmental variables (Taylor, 1992).
I. Antecedents: Events that occur just prior to the problem behavior and trigger an immediate reaction from the student.
Examples: Teasing by a peer
Directions by a teacher
Difficult work assignment
Student success is dependent upon the match between instructional tasks and a student's present level of performance.
II. Setting Events: Seating arrangements
Physical health of the student
Prior events

Effective Interventions are Based on a Thorough Understanding of the Problem

In order to produce meaningful long-term behavior change an intervention must directly address the function and contextual influences of the challenging behavior (Doyle, 1986).

Goal: replace the problem behaviors with socially acceptable alternatives that achieve the same outcomes.

Challenging behavior represent skill deficits, and effective interventions address both the acquisition of appropriate alternatives and the creation of an environment that is conducive to the performance of those alternatives. Effective intervention also aims to prevent the display of challenging behaviors by addressing the role that contextual factors play in the display of problem behaviors.

Behavior Support Plans are Guided by a Strong Value Base

All students are treated with the same dignity and respect. The appropriateness of an intervention is measured by its effectiveness and its social acceptability. No intervention should dehumanize, stigmatize, or cause pain, physical, or emotional distress.

The proposed discipline plan will work best if it is adaptive on a school wide basis. All principle stakeholders should have an active plan in developing the plan. In our review, the classroom plan presented could serve as a pilot program. Results and findings from a pilot program can be used in planning for the school wide plan. Components and strategies outlined in the classroom plan could be expanded school wide. Additionally, classroom ecology and group processes should be essential components of all discipline plans developed.

The Teaching Process Model

The teaching process model can be infused with either of the models previously discussed by using this model, teachers may be able to meet one of his/her primary instructional responsibilities to provide students with a learning environment that is conducive to achievement and free from disruptions, distractions, and threats to their safety and well being (Cangelosi, 2000). The following activities comprise the model.

1. *Determine Needs of Students.* This activity will include assessing the needs of students. Assessment devices such as observations, interviews, rating scales, checklists, self reports, and questionnaires may be employed.

2. *Determine Learning Goals.* Results from assessment data in step I should be used to plan group and individual activities to

correct, remediate or eradicate behavior problems, or to develop strategies to prevent them from occurring.

3. *Design Learning Activities.* Learning activities involves what a teacher plans for students to experience to assist them in achieving a learning goal. According to Cangelosi (2000) the times in the day when teacher intend to have students engage in learning activities are referred to as "allocated time." During this step activities should be designed to achieve the stated goals and objectives. An alternate approach that teachers may use is a classroom discipline plan.

4. *Prepare for Learning Activities.* Teachers must be prepared and organized to teach the activities. Appropriate physical and human resources as well as materials used in teaching the activities should be available.

5. *Conduct Learning Activities.* Learning activities should be designed to achieve the stated objectives and to increase students on-task-behavior for much as possible student should be directly involved in the activities.

6. *Evaluate Students' Achievement Goals.* Some evaluation strategies should be developed to determine how well the students have mastered the content. The difference between pre and post assessment should be conducted. In essence the initial knowledge that students bring to the learning activity should be compared when they have completed the activity. Both formative and summative evaluations may be conducted. Formative evaluations may be used to make decisions relevant to modifying learning activities, summative evaluations may be used to make periodic judgments on students progress and assist in providing grades.

The application of "The Teaching Process Model" requires no special training for the teacher. It is a systematical way for reducing behavior problems by keeping children on task. Research conducted by (Fisher, Berliner, Filby, Marliave, Cahen & Dishaw, 1980) Woolfolk, 1993; Kapos, 1995, 1998; National Commission on Excellence in Education, 1983; Santini, 1998, have all attested to value of increasing "allocated time." In summary, their research finding clearly indicated that when the proportion of "allocated time" that students spend engaged in learning activities increased, students' achievement of learning goals increases.

Summary

Research by Doyle (1979), Kounin (1970)*; Barker (1968) articulated that   student cooperation and involvement are essential in classroom ecology and group processes. The teacher's major function in this process assure that the group processes efficiently carried out by correcting and monitoring disruptive behaviors which may impede the group process or task completion. Doyle and Carter (1984) investigated the relationship between academic tasks and student involvement and classroom management. They observed a junior high school teacher and students in three classes taught by her for approximately three months. Major findings revealed that some student disrupted instruction by pretending to be confused by asking questions to slow down the instruction and attempting to change the assignments. When the teacher did not respond to the students question in a timely manner, many became angry. The teacher realized that in order to maintain order in the classroom, she had to address questions posed by the students.

The teacher should correlate principles of childhood development with his/her own beliefs relevant to how children learn. Next, various theories of learning and management models should be examined to determine which ones will be used.

As indicated a teacher may draw from several theories and models to construct her/his own model. A school wide discipline model should be the ultimate and for each school, once the effectiveness of a classroom model has been demonstrated. We have addressed in Chapters 3 – 9 specific ways and models which may be used to construct classroom in school wide discipline plan.

---

*For specific research strategies in group processes refer to: J.S. Kounin, (1970). Discipline and Group Management in Classrooms. New York: Rinehart & Winston.

Chapter 3

The Kounin Model

George R. Taylor

Introduction

Kounin summarized the affects of teachers reprimands on students behaviors. He referred to the process as the "ripple effect", when other students are adversely affected by the reprimand. The ripple effect may have negative effects on the teachers' efforts to maintain discipline in the classroom. Kounin (1970a) related teachers reprimands to desists, a process referred as remarks intended to stop inappropriate behaviors. Other research conducted by Kounin and his colleagues revealed that teachers who employed a technique refer to as "withitness," the ability to be aware of one's surroundings at all times; in essence the teacher is aware of what is going on in the classroom at all times, showed greater control over classroom management by using selected attention strategies to reduce potential behavior problems.

Components of Desists

Research conducted over a period of years by Kounin, Grump, & Ryan (1961) in a variety educational settings indicated that "desists" consist of three major characteristics: clarity, firmness, and roughness. Clarity refers to the amount of information the teacher provides students during remarks made to stop inappropriate behavior. Frequently teachers simply verbalize a command for students to stop the behavior without specifying the behavior, or not providing a method or instruction for stopping the inappropriate behavior. When teachers make clear their demands for a student to stop inappropriate behaviors, other children in the classroom tend to demonstrate the inappropriate behavior less.

Behavior problems can be significantly reduced if teachers can demonstrate to students that they can accurately detect classroom events.

The following conditions can demonstrate to students that teachers are employing withitness:

1.   When discipline problems occur, the teacher takes immediate steps to correct or eliminate the inappropriate behavior displayed by the students responsible for it, not the innocent student.
2.   When more than one discipline problems occur simultaneously, the teacher makes an assessment and deals with the more serious one first.
3.   Off-task behaviors are dealt with directly before they are modeled by other students (Kounin, 1970b). Kounin further believed that withitness is essential for success for classroom management.

Kounin (1970b) further articulated that student engagement and on-task behavior is partly governed by how well teachers move and coordinate activities between several activities. This strategy increases students involvement in learning activities in the following ways: (1) keeping students informed about their progress in lessons, (2) providing them with challenges at different points in the lesson, and (3) by involving them in a variety of learning activities. Students attention and engagement levels are kept at a minimum. Cangelosi (1990) wrote that students waiting to get busy develop their own devices for relieving their boredom, such as attention-getting disruptions and daydreaming.

Teachers who are firm in their remarks to students may provoke the ripple affect. The manner in which the teacher conveys his/her meaning to the student will determine the degree of the ripple affect. Kounin stated that firmness may be increased if the teacher:

1.   Stop talking and look at the student;
2.   Walks toward the student;
3.   Touches the student;
4.   Guides the student toward appropriate behavior.

Teachers who employ the above techniques to manage inappropriate behavior will have less impact upon correcting behavior than those employing clarity strategies.

Roughness has a different affect on changing inappropriate behavior than the two previous mentioned techniques. Roughness implies such teacher behaviors as expressing anger, making threats, or punishing. This form of "desists" does little to change inappropriate behavior. Roughness tend to upset and make children anxious when witnessing such behaviors. Research conducted by Kounin (1970a) found that this type of "desist" had no effect on the amount of inappropriate behavior shown by students.

Attributes of Using Desists

Research findings by Kounin (1970a) clearly showed that the type of setting in which desists occurred have different affects on changing inappropriate behavior. Subjects in experimental settings Kounin found that desists modified had different effects according to the grade level of students. In naturalist settings where students had been instructed by the same teacher over a period of time, modified characteristics made no difference in how they behaved. The study did reveal that the teacher's ability to accurately monitor what was occurring in the classroom was more important than issuing a "desist" to the student demonstrating inappropriate behavior. Factors such as withitness, correct targeting, correct timing, and overlapping were more important "desists" techniques than using clarity, firmness, and roughness in controlling behavior.

As indicated, withiness refers to how accurately the teacher monitors what is taking place in the class at all times. Children sometimes call teachers who use withitness techniques as having eyes in the back of their heads. This technique has proven successful in stopping students' inappropriate behavior from occurring. Kounin (1970b) conveyed that students need to be convinced that teachers are in control and are aware of what is going on in the classroom at all times.

Correct targeting behavior by teachers imply to what degree teachers identifies the students who is responsible for emitting the inappropriate behavior. Sometimes teachers only see a student reacting to another student's provocation, confronting such a student will normally result in additional provocations. To avoid this type of incident, teachers could initially get all of the facts. Correcting targeting behaviors may result in a teacher ignoring a more serious behavior problem and addressing one of a less serious nature. According to Kounin (1970b) the teacher is making a mistake in targeting. When teachers mistarget behaviors, students sometimes react with increased inappropriate behaviors.

Correct timing is of prime importance in correcting misbehavior. It involves the teacher choosing an appropriate time to issue a desist. It is also a critical aspect of withitness. If correct timing is not used effectively, more serious actions may need to be taken by the teacher to correct the misbehavior. By initially containing the behavior the teacher remains in control by not allowing the misbehavior to increase before it is desisted. Teachers should correct misbehaving students as quickly as possible by using desist techniques which are well timed and addressed to the student causing the misbehavior with firmness and clarity (Brophy & Good, 1986).

Overlapping involves teacher reacting to more than one problem at a time. Teachers need the competencies to react to more than one behavior problem at a time. This reaction will determine whether or not a specific desist technique will work effectively to manage or control the behavior problems. The type and nature of the situation will determine to some degree which type of "desists" technique to use. The following techniques may be used:

1. The teacher may allow one situation to continue and correct the other one;

2. Drop the learning activity and respond to the inappropriate behavior. This technique may cause some students to become distracted and loose interest.

3. The most effective technique is for the teacher to continue with the instruction and communicate with the misbehavior by looking at the student or make brief remarks and continue with instruction. This technique will not interfere with learning and other instructional activities performed by the teacher.

Coordinating Management

When students move around the classroom from one activity to another, the movement should be coordinated and directed by the teacher. Movement may be both physical and psychological and may cause misbehavior if routines have not been established. Kounin's research has show that important relationships were found between students' behavior and the maintenance of momentum within and between lessons. Smooth transitions tend to improve students' attention and promote task-oriented behavior. Kounin also identified jerkiness and slow downs as impeding smooth transitions. Jerkiness interrupts the flow of learning activities. They may be short, momentary interruptions or relatively long episodes.

In addition, other forms of jerkiness include stimulus boundedness, thrusts, dangles, truncations, and flip flops. Edwards (1997) wrote that teachers who are stimulus–bound seem drawn to unplanned and irrelevant stimuli. They react to or comment about almost any extraneous event coming to their attention. They are distracted from the ongoing activity and become preoccupied with superfluous events.

Thrust according to Gnagey (1975) is a sudden interruption of a learning activity with an irrelevant announcement, order, statement, or question that disrupts the instructional process. The intrusion is made without consideration for what students are doing. Dangles also disrupt the learning process. It occurs when a teacher who is instructing a student in one activity suddenly begins working with another student leaving the first student with no directions for proceeding. A truncation may be viewed as a long-lasting dangle, where the smoothness of a lesson is destroyed when it is abruptly dropped in favor of another activity. A flip flop also occur at transition points in a lesson when the teacher terminates one activity and then starts another, only to return to the original activity again (Edwards, 1987).

Strategies for Avoiding Slowdowns

Kounin (1970a) articulated that lesson momentum keeps student interested, involved, and well-behaved. When the teacher looses momentum management problems usually surface. A lack of momentum is known as a "slowdown." Slowdowns are unproductive, impede learning and reflect to students that time is wasted. Slowdowns may occur in the form of overdwelling results when teachers continue to focus exclusively on a single issue long after students have understood the points being advanced. It is commonly referred to as preaching, nagging, or admonishing children for displaying inappropriate behaviors. When teachers use overdwelling strategies, lesson continuity is destroyed and inappropriate behavior is encouraged. Fragmentation may take many forms, but usually occurs when teachers divide an activity into subdivisions which only a single unit is needed. An effective teacher manages movement in his/her classroom by keeping instructions moving smoothly and avoiding jerkiness and slowdowns.

Group Focus

When teachers work with the entire class, according to (Lewis, Shane, & Watson, 1996; Kounin, 1970a), they had fewer disruptions and their students learned more. This process is called group focus and requires the participation of students who are not engaged in reciting during a lesson. All students get a chance to test their abilities and skills. Strategies recommended by Kounin (1970a) to facilitate group focus include:

1.   Create suspense. Pause and look around before selecting a reciter, saying, "Let's see now, I need to find a person who appears to know the answer."

2.   Avoid naming the student who will be called on until the question is asked. Randomly pick students to answer questions. Avoid patterns that allow students to predict when they will be called on and therefore do not have to prepare an answer.

3.   Intersperse questions that call for all students to respond in unison with those that require individuals to answer. For a response in unison teachers might either have the whole group recite or ask all students who know an answer to raise their hands.

4.   Alert those students who are reciting at the moment to be prepared to react to the reciter's response. Students may be told to look for mistakes or to formulate differences of opinion.

5.   A teacher may ask, for example, "Who agrees with an answer? Ask another student, What do you think is the correct answer?" Students who are not performing at the moment are thus invited to maintain focus on the lesson along with the person who is reciting.

It is incumbent upon the teacher to insure that all students under his/her supervision to expose to and master all of the content taught. Strategies recommended by Kounin (1970a) appears worthly of mentioning for assisting students in mastering content and successfully managing classroom behavior:

1. Have children to display their work so that it can be critiqued.
2. Require students to recite their answers to questions in unison.
3. Involve other students in recitation.
4. Provide opportunities for students to demonstrate their skill or knowledge of the subject being recited.
5. During a recitation, circulation and check the work of children who are not reciting.
6. Check the performance of students while they are performing.
7. Ask all students to construct written responses and randomly choose some to give their responses.

Maintaining Interests of Children

When the teacher provides activities based upon interests of children, inappropriate behaviors are significantly reduced in the classroom. Programming the interest of children in the instructional program will provide a variety of learning activities and improve attention. Teachers may employ a variety of procedures and strategies to promote interests of children and reduce boredom such as making instruction functional and challenging, basing instruction on the abilities and disabilities of the group, present information and materials on a multi-sensory level, use different modes of presentation such as laboratories, lecture, role playing, cooperative groups, and debate groups are to name but a few.

Summary

The Kounin Model is designed to prevent discipline problems in the classroom. No strategies are provided for correcting behavioral problems in the classroom or on a school wide basis. It may be infused and integrated with other models discussed to correct behavior. The model is based upon empirical research and provides evidence that teachers' behaviors in the classroom may promote or hinder learning. It is not designed to help students to become responsible for the behaviors. The importance of timing in dealing with discipline problems is an important factor in the model. The model is not recommended to be employed to a broad range of classroom situations of teaching approaches, rather its effectiveness as classroom recitation sessions have been well documented.

Chapter 4

The Ginott Model

George R. Taylor

Overview

The Ginott Model is based upon interpersonal interaction between students and teachers. A proactive approach is recommended where students are made to feel accepted. There are constructed strategies for teachers to develop self-esteem, self-confidence and deemphasising fear, and frustration in the classroom. Ginott (1972) strongly endorses the concept that teachers should attack the problem not the child.

Labeling and Negative Criticism

Many teachers are not aware of the harmful affects of labeling and negatively criticizing children. Using labels to criticize children is self-defeating and damage their self-image (Kauffman, Wong, Lloyd, Hung & Pullen, 1991). The labels used frequently become a self-fulfilling prophecy. Children usually demonstrate behaviors characteristic of the labels associated with them. Labels manifest negative attitudes in children and they are difficult to erase. Ginott (1971) articulated that teachers should not criticize children, too much criticism is detrimental to their welfare and social growth, because it deflates self-esteem and interferes with learning. Ginott recommend that teacher should give suggestions and advise and make brief statements to students for improving their performances and seek their input and to correct behavior. Acknowledging students' feelings promote self-worth and confidence and provide an avenue for free expression.

Developing Independence in Students

Teachers should praise successful attempts by students and indicate an acceptance of their efforts. Ginott (1973) stated that students are dependent on us, and dependency breeds hostility. He further reported that by improving student-teacher relationships does not involve doing more for students, but rather assisting them in achieving greater independence.

Students need to be provided with opportunities to make as many choices as they are qualified to make; otherwise according to Ginott dependency will increase and dependency breeds hostility. Teachers must experiment with various ways of accepting students' autonomy in the classroom, by giving them choices relevant to classroom procedures.

Teachers must provide a classroom atmosphere where they will not have to give directives and order children around. They should describe the situation to them and leave children to make their own choices (Long, 1991). This approach promotes less defiance and increases relationship between children and teachers, promoting autonomy with student. Dependency also tends to promote indecisiveness and resentment. Independency leads to promote learning and positive behaviors among children (Ginott, 1972). The importance of trust between teachers and children are essential in promoting independency and positive behavior in the classroom.

Trust

Friedland (1999) wrote that educators must involve students so that they feel realistic ownership and empowerment as part of the learning process. It was further indicated that constantly controlling students and directing them to bend to our will is against developmental needs and creates a disinvitational climate, which may be counter productive in controlling inappropriate behavior. By a sense of trust between teacher and children a strong bond is developed which will motivate student to behave appropriately in the classroom. When students began to behave appropriately in the classroom, they have assumed responsibilities for their behaviors. The style and leadership ability of the teacher is necessary for children to independently control their behavior (Taylor, 1999).

Dealing with Feelings

Teachers according to Ginott (1973) should not attempt to assess students' feelings rather they should assist children in sorting out their feelings. Teachers should withhold their opinions and simply act as sounding boards. Ginott recommended that teachers paraphrase students' communication and indicate that they understand how the students feel.

Teachers need not accept what the students say as being true, but accept the expression of feeling and assist them in understanding that they or their feelings are not being rejected. When offering assistance to children assure them that they can not solve many of their own problems and that the teacher is readily available to support them. Children need to feel that they can depend upon the teacher to assist them when confronted with problems. If teachers do not assist children in solving their problems, they will attempt to solve them alone. Frequently, this approach will lead to inappropriate behaviors (Taylor, 1998).

Educators should permit children to express their feelings. According to Mountrose (1999) when children are not permitted to express their feelings, they are stored and buried in their sub-conscious minds. If teachers do not recognize these feelings, they maybe unleashed or directed toward inappropriate behaviors. When feelings are addressed children feel nurtured and recognized. Talking to children and assisting them in describing their feelings, aid in developing understanding and promote self-esteem. It also provides the opportunity for teachers to develop social skill to teach children how to scope successfully with their feelings by transforming inappropriate behaviors to appropriate behaviors (Vincent, 1990).

Praising Children

Praise is widely employed to motivate students, to achieve at their optimum level. Educators and parents frequently use this technique to recognize children's achievement, the successful completion or a task, or the demonstration of appropriate behavior. Kauffman, Mostert, Trent, and Hallahan (1998) contended that it is not enough just to make many positive statements and show approval to students, positive praise and attention must be contingent on the type of behavior children should demonstrate (Kohn, 1993).

Ginott's (1973) view of praise is somewhat different than the views discussed above. He believed that praise can be both destructive or productive, depending on how it is used. Additionally, he stated that evaluative praise can be destructive. To praise appropriately, teachers should tell students what they have accomplished and let them draw their own conclusions relevant to its value. It was also stated that praising students for their academic performance is a poor practice. Students who are publicly praised for high performance on a test and told how smart they are sometimes react negative to the praise because it embarrasses them and they may receive negative reactions from their peers. Teachers should use statements of appreciation instead of praise when assessing students' work and behaviors.

Causes of Inappropriate Behavior

The causes of inappropriate behaviors are many as discussed in Chapter 1. At this point a summary of causes of inappropriate behavior in the classroom will be outlined. Frequently, inappropriate behavior is caused by poorly defined rules and expectations of children. Children simply do not know how to adhere to the rules. Teacher must model and teach the rules and ensure that children know how to demonstrate them appropriately. The same analysis can be made for routines and structures within the classroom and school. An instructional plan based upon the needs, interests and abilities of children is essential for positive classroom management (Taylor, 1997).

Inappropriate Behavior and Punishment

When children commit inappropriate behaviors, one of the consequences of such behaviors is punishment and other forms of negative consequences. Punishment for inappropriate behavior may be accomplished by either withdrawing a positive reinforcer or employing aversive consequences, such as reprimands, isolation, or time out. Most school districts prohibit the use of pain consequences to correct inappropriate behaviors. Reprimands and some social isolation may be used carefully if they do not cause any undue stress on children.

Social isolation may take many forms, however, for most teachers it is frequently referred to as "timeout". Timeout may be interpreted as timeout from positive reinforcement, in essence it is an interval during which positive reinforcement cannot be obtained. Time out does not necessary mean isolation from the group. It may simply restrict the student from interacting with the group and receiving positive rewards. Placing children in isolated rooms without supervision is highly discouraged.   Additional pre long "timeout" periods are not recommended. It is recommended that five (5) minute periods be used, and that timeout place offer little reinforcement for the student. Ginott (1973) does not support the use of punishment. He feels punishment increases rather than decreases inappropriate behavior. Refer to Chapter 6 for additional details on behavior modification techniques.

Controlling Inappropriate Behavior

Many types of inappropriate behaviors irritate teachers and cause them to respond negatively to many situations, such as threats, rudeness, over reacting and punishing children. According to the Ginott Model, none of the above negative behaviors displayed by teachers are productive and do nothing to eliminate the behavior. Teachers must find effective alternative to punishment. Ginott stated that punishment is more likely to enrage students and significantly impede their learning. They frequently become hostile, and full of anger. Effective discipline requires teachers to act with kindness and patience. Good discipline requires a great deal of self-control on the part of the teacher. When teachers react in a negative way, children will defy them. When they exhibit love, compassion and understanding, children usually respond positively. Discipline with punishment usually lead to various degrees of physical force and promote increased inappropriate behaviors. When students defy teachers they are seeking attention and rewards through teachers' verbal and physical reactions. Once the cycle starts it is difficult to control. Punishment does not stop inappropriate behavior, it simply makes students more skillful in covering up their behavior (Taylor, 1998). Negative remarks from teachers can also have adverse affects on students' behaviors.

Kauffman, Mostert, Trent & Hallahan (1998) firmly believed that negative teacher talk promotes inappropriate behaviors in children. The authors indicated that constant negativity or belittling talk are unlikely to convince a student to improve his/her behavior, rather it may be a personal attack of the student's self-esteem. Van Horn (1992) supported the statement by indicating that students feel less defensive and more willing to engage in learning when teachers do not use negative or judgmental language. Judgmental language that focuses on personalities is particularly detrimental to a climate of cooperation. Teachers should communicate to students descriptions of situations and behaviors, but never make value judgments about children.

Inappropriate behaviors of students, if at all possible, should not be addressed before peers. Appropriate timing, voice control and position near the student are also important factors that teachers could employ when correcting inappropriate behaviors (Taylor, 1999).

Kaufman, Mostert, Trent & Hallahan recommended that teachers and educators should have the following objectives in mind when communicating to students concerning inappropriate behaviors:
1.   Indicate clearly that the behavior is unacceptable;
2.   Indicate clearly what is expected from the student; and
3.   Model and demonstrate to the students acceptable behavior as well as expectations and consequences of inappropriate behaviors.

Summary

The Ginott Model does not contain a plan or strategies for preventing behavior problems, rather it proposes the need for teachers to be loving, warm, and patient. Ginott (1973) articulated that the approach will prevent many discipline problems from occurring. The model also does not include any strategies for school wide discipline. Accordingly, if teachers apply their recommendations there will be no need for a school wide plan. The model appears to be more child-centered than behavioral.

The Model's main focus is on the development of the self-concept, which is essential in avoiding rebellion in children. This approach promotes positive relations between teachers and students. Student autonomy is encouraged by permitting them to make choices. There are no comprehensive set of principles to apply, however, a long list of dos and don'ts are listed, which may prevent many teachers from using the model.

Chapter 5

The Glasser Classroom Model

Lois Nixon

Overview

The Glasser Model (1986) is similar to the Dreikurs Model (1968) in that both models attempt to satisfy the basic needs of students through emphasizing their self worth. Both models advocate that the coercion-punishment should be replaced, and they proposed that promoting love and the self worth of students can be attained through classroom meetings. Such meetings are designed to find solutions to behavior problems, as well as students learning to take responsibility for their own behavior and social development. Teachers must take an active part in conducting classroom meetings. They must ensure that all children participate, keep children on task, and provide leadership. The organization of the classroom for classroom meetings must be considered by the teacher, as well as the classroom climate, identifying problems, finding alternate ways of solving behavior problems, following and evaluating progress (Fulk, 1997).

This model by Glasser is built on the child-center approach and designed to assist children in developing self-management skills (Kohn, 1996; Nodding, 1992; and Oakes & Lipton, 1999). These authors have enumerated principles that teachers may employ in using the model:
1.   Act in ways that are socially just;
2.   Develop authentic relationship free of power and control;
3.   Allow students to construct moral meaning;
4.   Limit structure and procedures;
5.   Give students a say and have them solve problems together.

Teachers must model ways of demonstrating these principles by creating classroom environments, which promote participation and trust.

Refer to Kohn (1996)* strategies for dealing with disruptive or misbehaving students.

Glasser (1969) recommends using two strategies to assist students in managing their behaviors:

1. Reality therapy. This therapy is designed to help students: a) recognize and describe their behaviors; b) identify the consequences of their behaviors; c) make value judgments relevant to the consequences of the unwanted behaviors; and d) formulate plans to eliminate inappropriate behaviors.

2. Control theory. This theory is premised upon providing opportunities in the classroom for students to meet their basic needs by teachers providing an atmosphere where by students can control and self correct their behaviors. Balancing needs of children is a vital part of control theory. Glasser (1984) recommends teaching children to balance their needs by having them give up some control in favor of developing a social relationship. The need for freedom and control must also be balanced. Conflicts between freedom and control may constitute a problem when children want freedom, but are not willing to grant the same freedoms they seek to others.

In Glasser's opinion when teachers employ these strategies in their classroom, inappropriate behaviors can be eliminated. His principles of classroom control is based upon children having successful social relationships. He supports the notion that social and psychological problems are an out growth of bad decisions made about social relationships. In appropriate social relationships can be replaced with socially acceptable ones. This theory also purports that the basic human needs of students must be considered, students must feel loved and accepted, and they must be given opportunities to self-correct their own behaviors.

Reality Therapy

Reality therapy is designed to assist students in recognizing and correcting their behaviors. When inappropriate behaviors have been displayed in the classroom, students are required to develop a plan to correct their behaviors. Interviews are also used to assist students in

---

*A. Kohn (1996). Beyond discipline: Compliance to community. Alexandria, VA: Association for Supervision and Curriculum Development.

correcting inappropriate behaviors, providing that a positive rapport has been established (Glasser, 1969). The major purposes of the behavioral plan and the interview are to: 1) assist students in identifying the inappropriate behaviors, 2) assist students in identifying consequences of negative behaviors, 3) assist students in making value judgments about their behaviors and their consequences, 4) assist students in implementing their behavioral plans or suffer the consequences already agreed upon during the interview.

Identify Inappropriate Behaviors

Before developing a behavioral plan or interviewing students who engage in inappropriate behaviors, the first step in reality therapy is for the teacher to identify the source of the behavior. In some instances other school personnel may need to be consulted, such as the social worker or the school psychologist. It is highly recommended that the teacher confer with the parents, as well (Taylor, 1999, 2000). We have indicated in Chapter 13 the value of parental involvement in changing negative behaviors. Students tend to shift blame or not claim behavioral acts. Teachers must assist students in owning up to their behaviors. Glasser (1969) recommends that no attempt should be made to judge the behavior as being good or bad. Students should be encouraged to state or describe their behaviors in their own words. During this process, the teacher should pose questions which will help the student clarify his/her behavior. Students will frequently not accept blame for the behavior, in this case the teacher may simply ask the student to describe his/her involvement in the incident. The teacher must assess the authenticity of the student's responses.

Identifying Consequences

Once the inappropriate behaviors have been identified, the next step in reality therapy is to identify the consequences of inappropriate behaviors with input from the student concerning the alleged behavior. An interview or a one-to-one discussion is needed with the student, the teacher may need to clarify certain aspects of the behaviors as well as making sure that the student understand the consequences of the behavior and to assess whether or not the student consider his/her behavior to be inappropriate. If the student decides that his/her behavior is inappropriate, and desires to avoid the consequences associated with the behavior, a behavioral plan may be developed to resolve the behavior or the problems associated with it. Teachers should provide clues to assist students in developing plans. Glasser (1989) articulated that students must make value judgments about their behavior if they are to affect change. Teachers must maintain an open and positive approach toward negative attitudes displayed by the student, and should not succumb by reacting to deviant behaviors displayed by the student.

Time Out

Time out is used in reality therapy to remove or isolate a child from the classroom when he/she refuse to follow class rules. Unlike traditional time-out in behavioral programs, reality therapy time-out is not meant to be punitive, rather it is used to provide time for students to develop a workable plan for solving their problems before returning to the classroom. A time out place should be created in the classroom and monitored by the teacher or another school personnel. The plan may be considered as a contract between the child and the teacher. If any part of the plan is not met, the students should be recycled through the steps in reality therapy. Additionally, they may be required to suffer the consequences of their behaviors, which standards they assisted in developing (Glasser, 1989).

Control Theory

Control theory according to Glasser (1984) is compatible with reality therapy. He viewed control theory and extension of reality therapy, with control theory designed to prevent behavior problems and reality therapy designed to correct behavior problems. Several basic needs are associated with control theory. They are love, control, freedom, and fun. Glasser (19484) recommends that teacher teach those basic human needs to children.

Love

All children need love and acceptance by others. If the need for love and acceptance is not realized by children, they will frequently resort to inappropriate behaviors to receive attention. Approval from others can usually satisfy the child's need for love and acceptance. Children will be seen and heard, if they are lonely, not considered part of the group, not involved in group activities, not chosen to participate in group activities, they may behave aggressively to be accepted. Teachers should ensure that all children under their supervision are frequently told that they are love and accepted. Strategies should be developed to teach children how to love and accept others (Taylor, 2000).

Control

Teachers who attempt to control children when they seek to be independent by making choices encourage children to rebel against authority. Teachers using the approach to deny children to satisfy their needs and punish them for making choices, usually increase rebellion and reinforce the behavior as a reaction to teacher control (Kohn, 1993).

Edwards (1997) states that the need to control cannot simply be renounced, it is a legitimate need. However, the way in which control is exercised must usually be modified. People basically use control to manipulate the environment of others so as to satisfy their needs. The use of control is appropriate so long as others can satisfy their needs. Children's efforts to obtain control are often awkward and do not consider the feeling of others. Additionally, Edwards (1997) states that teachers might react negatively to students' efforts to manage themselves. They assume that students are too immature to exercise control over their actions. When teachers intervene to change behaviors sometimes children react angrily because they want to make decisions on their own concerning behaviors.

Freedom

In control theory the need for children to control their own behaviors and lives are stressed. When children attempt to control their own lives conflict between them and their teacher usually pursue, because many teachers see these behaviors as a direct threat to their authority. Some teachers doubt whether or not students are mature enough to act responsibly when given complete freedom to make decisions. Children must earn the right to exercise control over their lives. It is incumbent upon the teacher to provide decision-making strategies which will gradually increase the freedom of students as they demonstrate how to use them humanly in making valid decisions concerning classroom structure and management. Some cautions are in order when providing freedom to children. Edward (1997) summarizes them as follows:
1. Providing freedom to children is no guarantee that children will use it responsibly;
2. Unrestrained freedom can cause chaos;
3. If too much teacher control is exercised, rebellion may occur;
4. Teachers need to provide freedom gradually as children demonstrate the ability to govern themselves;
5. Teachers must offer children choices and at the same time teach about the consequences of those choices;
6. Children must be taught the freedom to exists only when consequences are taken into consideration, ignoring consequences will restrict or eliminate the freedom they seek.

Fun

The need to have fun is essential in child development and learning. Glasser (1984) believes that fun is a basic as any other human need for children. The need for fun activities infused within the curriculum of the school is needed to provide pleasure to learning. Students should take pleasure in what they are learning, unfortunately this concept is not fully endorsed by most schools. Many school operate on the premise that having fun is not learning and should be hard work. Fun is essential in developing a well-rounded functional child. When children are having fun with instruction, many of the difficult and abstract concepts needed to master the curriculum can be easily understood and realized.

The Quality School Model

Glasser (1984) contends that a radical restructuring of the school is necessary before his model can be successfully implemented. He maintained that the school must realize that students cannot deny their needs. The school has often overlooked or has not considered satisfying the needs of students. Evidence of the school not meeting the needs of students are evident in low achievement and dropout rates. Additionally, ignoring basic needs of students according to Glasser has resulted in increased discipline problems in the school.

In order to revert the after mentioned, Glasser (1990) has created "The Quality School Model". In his model, Glasser criticized the school for accepting work below standard. He believed by the school accepting poor work quality, students will not be motivated to learn unless they believe that there is quality in the work assigned. Glasser formerly believed that many of discipline problems defined by the school are school management problems which do not address the human needs of students. Educators must allow for considerable variation in how students satisfy their needs based upon their individual needs and learning styles (Taylor, 1999). Much of the work in "The Quality School Model" should be done in groups or individually where high quality work is stressed. In a quality school, a low grade is considered temporary until the problem is resolved through a team effort involving student and teacher.

Proactive Strategies

Through employing proactive strategies such as social-problem-solving meetings, open-ended meetings and educational diagnosis meetings, Glasser (1969) pinpoints that the basic needs of most children can be met and discipline problems significantly reduced. Social-problem-solving meetings are designed to solve problems as a class. Issues, standards and consequences are established and agreed upon. Curriculum issues are resolved through open-ended meetings. Curriculum content, presentation and tasks are discussed and agreed upon. County and state mandated requirements are not negotiated. Students can evaluate their educational experiences through the use of educational diagnosis meetings. Strategies for improving learning as well as problems in achieving standards are articulated.

Glasser (1969) has provided detail steps he believes will improve discipline in the schools. They will only be summarized at this point. For specific details refer to "Schools with Failure."*

1. Determine as a class what the goals of instruction will be. Teachers should provide students with sufficient information to make relevant decisions.

2. Formulate classroom rules which correlates and support achievement of the specified goals stated above.

3. Permit students to be involved in making suggestions relevant to classroom operations that they believe will promote a productive learning environment. Suggestions concerning the amount of homework, examinations, and standards for written work, etc. can all be made and discussed by students.

4. Achieve commitment by all students for goals, rules and procedures decided on. Total support relevant to the above should receive full support by the entire class. Students should be provided an opportunity to suggest changes that they think should be made.

Decide on the consequences that should be applied for any inappropriate behavior. Teachers should remind students of the previously agreed consequences of any infractions of the goals, rules, and procedures, and instruct students to accept ownership for consequences and not consider them as punishment.

Summary

Significant research has been conducted on Glasser Theory and Model for improving discipline in the classroom. He has always advocated the involvement of students in the formulation of goals, rules and procedures in classroom. He further supports the notion that students must take ownership of their behaviors, as well as denouncing the Boss-Management Model. Improved social relationships are an essential component or his model. Key points in his model are summarized:

1. Assist in reducing inappropriate behavior.
2. Identify the consequences of behavior.

---

*Glasser, W. (1969). Schools without failure. New York: Harper & Row.

3.   Make value judgments about behaviors and their consequences.
4.   Create a behavioral plan to eliminate negative behavior.
5.   Assist in helping student satisfy their basic human needs in a meaningful and socially accepted way.
6.   Maintain a balance between meeting one's needs and impact they may have on the needs of others.
7.   Poor achievement levels in schools may be attributed to poorly designed education rather than to discipline problems.
8.   A quality school model is designed to satisfy students' needs, promote student's involvement and ownership, promote group and individual work and avoid coercion.

Chapter 6

Behavioral Management Strategies

Lois Nixon

Introduction

Behavior modification techniques may be characterized as another form of individualized instruction. These may be adapted to individuals and designed to change unacceptable behaviors in several areas. They are frequently referred as the application of psychological principles in changing behaviors or organisms. Additionally, they provide some objective evaluation of the behavior to be changed.

Behavior modification techniques have been applied with great success in a wide range of problems dealing with inappropriate behaviors (Taylor, 2001). Successful programs have been developed in the areas of social behavior, academic achievement, motor development, and a variety of other behaviors. Bandura (1969) indicated that behavior includes a complexity of observable and potentially measurable activities, including motor, cognitive, and physiological classes of responses.

Walker, Horner, Suqai, Bullis, Spraque, Bricker, and Kaufman (1996) along with Reavis, Kukic, Jenson, Morgan, Andrews, and Fister (1996) have concluded that a behavior modification system has tremendous potential for working with exceptional individuals. Educators who employ behavior modification techniques are using an effective strategy; however, they are seldom provided with sufficient guidance as to when the approach should be used, for whom, by whom, and toward what end.

Kazid (1973) wrote that behavior modification programs can be no more successful than the staff who utilizes them. He offered four points which should be considered before implementing a program: 1) staff competencies needed to administer the program, 2) strategies required for developing behaviors in clients which are not controlled by the presence of the staff, 3) techniques for augmenting the performance of intractable clients, and 4) methods for the maintenance of client behaviors after the behavior program has terminated. In essence, certain personnel and facilities should be available before educators attempt to develop behavior modification strategy. They need to know and explore the limitations and liabilities of the strategy.

On the other hand, current literature abounds with studies reporting on the successful application of behavior modification techniques with individuals.   The basic principles of behavior modification are neither new nor unique, but the systematic application of its fundamentals to specific problems of human behavior has recently been given increased attention by professionals in the field of education. Principles of direct observation, continuous measurement, and systematic manipulation of the environment were preached early in the nineteenth century; and more recently, behavior modification has received increasing attention, especially within special education during the last decade. This increased attention within special education is, in part, because of the emphasis on task analysis and learning theory (Walker, 1997; Christopolos & Valletutti, 1969; Lovith, 1970; Breen & Fiedler, 1996; Algozzine, 1991; Kaufman, et al., 1998).

Historical Overview

According to Macmillan and Forness (1970), the use of the behavior modification strategy may be traced to 1800 when Itard used reinforcement techniques with the wild boy Victor. The strategy was further refined by Sequin, and during the 1930s and 1940s, psychologists worked to improve the techniques and broaden the application of conditioning principles. During this time span, experiments were mostly confined to the laboratory setting with emphasis on animals and on humans with severe emotional or mental conditions.   Skinner's publications concerning animal behavior gave added impetus to the movement.   Efforts were then expanded to apply the principles of reinforcement to a wide range of behavior problems.

The 1960s brought an increase in the frequency of use of behavior modification principles. Macmillan and Forness (1970) reported that researchers launched investigations into several areas of human behavior.   Nelsen, Lott and Glenn (1993) focused attention on the interaction between a child and his/her learning environment. Jackson and Owens (1999) work focused on developing special environments and stress management for emotionally disturbed. Bandura (1969) concluded experiments with modeling techniques.

Around the middle of the present decade, behavior modification was becoming increasingly accepted as a strategy, which had particular values for educating exceptional individuals. More recently, Goodall (1972) remarked that behavior modifiers or controllers have increasingly moved away from laboratory-like settings of mental hospitals, correctional institutions, and special classrooms and have been applied in public schools, halfway houses, private homes, and community health centers.

Modifying behavior has always been one of the principal goals of educational programs for individuals. According to Christopolos and Valletutti (1969) there is nothing radically new about behavior modification. What does appear to be innovative in the field is the emphasis on evaluation or measurement techniques to determine how effectively behavior is actually modified in the direction identified by the educator. These authors outlined and discussed three aspects related to the behavior modification trend: 1) information about the child, 2) information about the task, and 3) information about the management process. It was concluded that only through the integration of the above aspects of behavior modification could curriculum development truly become a functional tool in the service of educators. Systematic observations may provide information needed to construct an effective behavior modification program.

Role of Observation

Observation is the primary source for determining what behaviors patterns exist at various stages in a program as well as what degree of reinforcement is in the natural environment. Observational data are also employed to monitor the implementation of a behavior modification program in addition to identify personal preferences among reinforcers used in the program. Observations can provide much information about effective reinforcement patterns as well as the kinds of behaviors that should be reinforced.

Records from behavior modification will reflect the frequencies on time rates of specific types of behaviors. Precise information on a child's behavior in several academic areas will be revealed. Teachers may use this information to diagnosis and sequence the instructional program for children. These records may be used diagnostically to assist teachers in adapting and modifying resources and expectancies of instruction to a child's preference.

Defining Behavior Modification

Behavior modification is the application of behavioral analysis to correct an individual's maladaptive behavior by determining with great precision which procedures are effective and which ones are not. According to Krasner and Ullman (1965) the term denotes a specific theoretical position in regard to changing behavior. The strategy consists essentially of introducing reinforcement contingencies, which encourage the emergence of predetermined response patterns. Both classical and operant conditioning may be employed. The former is achieved by pairing the reinforcer with a stimulus; the latter by making the reinforcer contingent upon a response. Kessler (1966) reflected that in classical conditioning, stimuli are associated with an unconditioned response, whereas in operant conditioning, the response operates on the environment to produce certain results. The organism is not a passive participant in the learning process as in conditioning.

Behavior modification techniques include a variety of approaches such as operant conditioning, contingency management, behavioral modeling., role playing, and other approaches designed to alter maladaptive behavior. In operant conditioning, desired behaviors are reinforced in an attempt to establish new operant behavior. Continuous reinforcement implies reinforcement after each occurrence of the desired response. Intermittent schedules may be one of several types: 1) fixed interval schedule, 2) variable interval schedule, 3) fixed ratio schedule, and 4) variable ratio schedule.

Fixed Interval Schedule

Contingency contracting is that behavior modification strategy wherein the subject knows that a particular reward depends upon the completion of a certain task or tasks. The individual is rewarded if he/she successfully completes his/her part of the contract. Modeling refers to copying socially acceptable behaviors. This technique is based upon the premise that most behavior can be imitated by the students if they are given a correct model to follow.

Behavior strategy may operate on the following techniques: 1) positive reinforcement contingencies, 2) negative reinforcement contingencies, and 3) a combination of positive and negative reinforcement contingencies. Regardless of the type of reinforcement employed, it is imperative that the reinforcement be scheduled systematically. Initially, the reinforcement should be given immediately after the behavioral act; subsequent reinforcement schedules may be changed depending upon the abilities of the individual. It is of prime importance that the reinforcement scheduled be consistent if the behavior modification strategy is to be successful in changing behavior. A summary of the procedures to employ are summarized below:

1.   The behavior or behaviors must be clearly defined. Appropriate classroom behavior, for example, might include reading an assignment, attending to the teacher, looking toward a reciting student, or responding to a teacher's questions.

2.   The reinforcer should be a natural consequence or paired with one. Nature reinforcers are present in the child is immediate environment, and significant influence behaviors of children. These reinforcers frequently include praise, recognition, and granting physical activities for the exchange of positive behaviors.

3.   Entitlements should be respected. There are certain activities in which children should be entitled to regardless of how they behave, these entitlements include, recess, and other classroom privileges. This is a point or contention with some teachers, some teachers believe that children should be denied entitlements, if their behaviors are not appropriate. In our view, activities and entitlements should not be based upon children demonstrating appropriate behaviors and should not be employed to deny entitlements to children who misbehave.

4.   Once the behavior is clearly defined, the operant or baseline level of the behavior is recorded. The level of the behavior must be measured as it is occurring before any attempts are made to change the behavior.

5.   The experimental procedures are then instituted. Attempts are made to modify the behavior by rearranging the consequences which follow the behavior.

6.   The recording of the behavior is then continued. This provides continuous feedback as to the effectiveness of the modification and indicates if further modification procedures are necessary.

7.   The next step is to carry out a scientific verification by instituting a reversal or by using a multiple-baseline design. A reversal design is one in which experimental procedures are discontinued briefly so that baseline conditions are in effect once again. If the behavior reverts to its former level, experimental conditions are reinstituted. If this again results in a change, a cause and effect relationship has been demonstrated. This change or effect may be the result of a negative or positive reinforcer.

Negative Reinforcement

Negative reinforcement and punishment are not synonymous. Negative reinforcement implies that an individual in authority reinforces behavior by removing something unpleasant, and permits a child to escape or avoid a negative consequences. On the other hand punishment denotes providing a consequence that decreases the likelihood that a behavior will be reported. The most effective punishment involves withholding or withdrawing a positive reinforcer. Both negative reinforcement and punishment are not recommended for use in the classroom, because it relies upon using negative consequences, and negative consequences may not promote affective learning and behavior in the classroom.

Positive Reinforcement

According to Kauffman, Mostert, Trent, and Hallahan (1998), positive reinforcement is the staple of good behavior management, and it is a concept with which teachers are familiar. Appropriate and positive behaviors of children are rewarded. Positive reinforcement appears to promote appropriate behavior if administered properly. Educators are not always successful in using positive reinforcement because they do not adhere to guidelines in using it effectively. Some recommended guidelines for teachers and educators to employ:

1. The consequence used should be a positive reinforcer for the student. The consequence must meet the individual needs and interests of the student. Consequently, educators must assess and observe students to determine their needs and interests.
2. The reward should depend on the student demonstrating the appropriate behavior that the teacher is attempting to increase, and be reinforcements that the teacher can control and administer.
3. The reinforcer should be available soon after the student demonstrates the appropriate behavior. Teachers must recognize the importance of rewarding students promptly when using positive reinforcement.
4. Provide an appropriate unit or reward for the expected unit of behavior. Rewards and reinforcers should be matched until the behaviors have been demonstrated. Children should know what reinforcers and rewards are given for certain positive behaviors. All positive behaviors should not receive the same rewards.

Goal Determination in a Behavior Modification Strategy

Goals should come first, not the methods for assessing progress towards the goals. Goals however, are derived primarily from measures. In the determination of adequate behavioral objectives, one of the steps in a behavior modification strategy requires that a teacher work with both short and long range objectives. Without the association between short and long range objectives, the objectives themselves become fractional bits of behavior with little relationship to the process of educational development.

Goal determination in behavior modification research tends to indicate the following: 1) behavior modification cannot be arbitrarily applied because the strategy does not provide teachers with educational goals or philosophies, 2) behavior modification describes learning as a change in observable behavior, disregarding the entire range of covert and unobserved learning, 3) the use of the strategy limits the target behavior to precise, quantifiable, and measurable behaviors, ignoring less easily defined and difficult to measure behaviors, and 4) the strategy concentrates almost entirely non-objective measurements, not recognizing the subjective realm of human functioning.

Behavior modification techniques have proven extremely successful in eliminating maladaptive behavior in children with behavioral disorders (Algozzine, 1991; Breen & Fiedler, 1996). Some of the benefits of applying behavior modification for educational purposes:

- The most significant contribution is that behavior modification helps make education more of a science. It provides a language, including operationally defined terms, which makes precise communication possible. Precise communication helps make possible the replication of studies and the validation of results.
- By utilizing behavior modification techniques, the educator is better prepared to control behavior. Having command of the group or individuals in one way or another guarantee freedom from the disciplinarian role. Consequently, concern can more appropriately focus on educational programming.
- Any academic subject or problem area can be approached with behavior modification techniques. The contingencies determining the results can be identified whether the task includes reading, writing, arithmetic, or sitting in a seat ready for work. The virtually unlimited potentials for application to a wide range of tasks make it an extremely valuable tool for all educators (Taylor, 2001).

Behavioral and Emotional and Social Development

Behavior – How a student conducts himself or herself in school – is often a key factor in educational performance. Certainly, behavior that is off-target academically or socially – inattention, being out of seat, talking too much, hitting or biting, skipping school – can detract from learning. When a student's behavior appears to be interfering with school performance and relationships with others, or when that behavior is maladaptive, bizarre, or dangerous, it becomes important to assess the student's behavior well as his or her emotional and social development. The need to take an ecological perspective when assessing a student's nonacademic behaviors in order to obtain a complete picture and examine the relationship between the behavior and environment is highly recommended.

Negative or inappropriate behaviors may occur for different reasons. One child may be disruptive in class because of attention deficit disorder. A second child may exhibit similar behaviors due to a mental illness, while another's inappropriate behavior may be linked to environmental factors such as his or her parents' recent divorce. Still another child may be disruptive only in one or two classes, for reasons associated with the way instruction is organized for something in that environment which the student finds disturbing. Thus, identifying why a child is exhibiting certain behaviors is an important part of the assessment process. The reasons why, if they can be determined, will influence whether or not the child is determined eligible for special education services and if so, will certainly affect the nature of decisions made regarding educational and other interventions (Taylor, 1998).

Effective interventions are based on a thorough understanding of the problem behavior. In order to produce meaningful long-term behavior change, an intervention must directly address the function and contextual influences of the challenging behavior. Challenging behaviors represent skill deficits, and effective interventions address both the acquisition of appropriate alternatives and the creation of an environment that is conducive to the performance of those alternatives. Effective intervention also aims to prevent the display of challenging behavior by addressing the role that contextual factors play in the display of problem behaviors.

Changing problem behaviors to socially accepted alternatives require that systematic steps be in place before the behavioral intervention is attempted (Brendtro & Long, 1995). Table 1 reflects recommended steps and the process to employ in dealing with problem behaviors. The process begins with identifying the target behavior in question, through evaluating the effectiveness of the program.

Table 6.1
Steps in Changing Negative Behaviors

Steps	Strategies
1	Identify the behavior you wish to change to decrease a problem behavior or increase a positive behavior. Pinpoint the behavior by being as specific as possible (i.e., hitting peers during play or at snack times).
2	Write down the goal you wish to achieve. For example, decrease the number of hitting behaviors towards peers during play or snack times.
3	List the steps you need to reach the goal (i.e., decreasing the hitting behaviors during snack times, decreasing the behaviors during play times), eliminating hitting behaviors during snack or play times. Reaching a goal via several small steps is usually more successful than attempting to achieve a goal in a single step, especially for young children.
4	Establish a baseline (how often the behavior occurs now) by counting the frequency of the behavior during snack or play times for a period of 3 – 4 consecutive days. Record the frequency on a chart that is easily accessible. Golf counters work great for charting the frequency of behaviors.
5	Decide on the method and type of chart you will use for recording the behavior you are attempting to change.
6	Evaluate the effectiveness of your behavior management program by recording the child's frequency of targeted behavior over the set period of time to determine if there is a decrease in frequency compared to the frequency of these behaviors recorded on your original baseline. If the behavior is decreasing in frequency, your methods and consequences are appropriate. If not, you will need to go back to Step 5 and make changes.

Limitations of a Behavior Modification Strategy

Behavior modification techniques provide systematic procedures which teachers may implement to change or modify deviant behavior and encourage more acceptable behavior. Skeptical, cautious acceptance and application are certainly indicated. Behavioral modification techniques are themselves morally blind. Some of the limitations to the behavioral approach: 1) the behavioral approach treats only the symptoms and not their causes, 2) it stresses remediation and minimized prevention, 3) behavioral problems cannot be nullified by a strategy which fails to penetrate environmental or psychology roots, 4) there is no transferable value because out-of-classroom behavior is not affected, and 5) self-discipline is devalued in favor of extrinsic management.

Teachers are often told to use a positive approach to influence behavior. The danger inherent in this approach is that rewards may impede natural motivation. Better management would help students feel the satisfaction inherent in doing good work for its own sake. Another danger arises when jealousy of the award sets children apart. When this occurs, those who are given an award may be treated as the "teacher's pet," thus, interfering with their social relationships with peers. In cases such as this, receiving an award becomes an unpleasant experience. A third danger is when the reward loses most of its value because it can be attained by only a few and is beyond the reach of most. The use of trinkets, food, and small toys may be ineffective for holding children at a task for any considerable length of time because of changes in the child's environment.

As concern increases with accountability and as the necessity for evaluation increases, another potential source of misuse of a behavior modification strategy is in the area of goal determination. Behaviorally-oriented educators stressed the setting of specific behavioral objectives to determine the direction for effort, and to provide precise means for evaluating that effort (Nelson, et al., 1998; Thompson & Walter, 1999). A dangerous potential is implicit in this desire for accountability and measurability – the situation whereby that which is measurable becomes the goal. The unfortunate situation thus arises in education, i.e., that it may become more rewarding for centers to teach that which is readily measured. Behaviors, which are not easily quantified, particularly those in the effective domain, may thus be excluded from the realm of desirable educational goals.

An approach that does not consider the whole child holds some portents for special education in that it considers the special individual as a collection of indiscrete and unrelated fractions. The basic assumptions underlying the development and utilization of fractional approaches is that human activity may be successfully separated into specific entities, being essentially independent and capable of being individually evaluated and treated. Human behavior is too complex to justify a fractional approach to behavior analysis; a systematic plan is needed. A school-wide approach appears to be an effective strategy to employ.

Discipline has been a major problem facing public schools for several decades. Many individuals have not responded effectively to traditional measures to learn self-discipline. Behavioral management techniques have been integrated into school-wide discipline plans. These techniques are designed to improve student self-control and responsibility through providing preventive strategies other than punishment (Research Connections in Special Education, 1997).

Designing a School-Wide Behavioral Management Plan

A large percentage of behavioral problems may be prevented by a school-wide discipline plan, which is implemented and supported by staff members, administrators, and family members (Nelson, Crabtree, Marchand, Martella & Martella, 1998). Consistent school-wide behavioral expectations for various activities and settings need to be established and taught. These expectations should reflect the school community's mission statement and discipline philosophy. The School Wide Discipline Plan includes the following elements:

1. Total staff commitment to the school-wide discipline philosophy toward managing behaviors.
2. School wide rules clearly defined and supported by the staff.
3. Common area routines and consequences for breaking rules
4. Plan for teaching rules and procedures and other social skills.
5. System for recognizing expected behaviors.
6. Description of consistent consequences for infractions.
7. Emergency procedures to obtain immediate in-school assistance.
8. System for communication.
9. Plan for training (Cheney, Barringer, Upham & Manning, 1995; Colvin, Kameenul & Sugia, 1993, Jones, 1993; Sugia & Pruitt, 1993).

Most students will follow the plan and respond with improved behavior if the following are implemented:

1. School and classroom climates are positive and safe and all stakeholders endorse the plan.
2. Staff personal skills should be realistic, competent, and unified in solving problems.
3. Rules should be systematically taught and correlated with the schools mission. They should be clear, fair, and the consequences of behavior fully understood by the pupils.
4. Behavior principle of behavioral management should be understood and practiced by all staff members.

5.   Parental and student support are essential to any success, parents must be fully apprised of the program, the rules and consequences of noncompliance. They should be totally involved from planning to implementing the behavioral strategy. They are powerful "significant others" for their children.

6.   Shared responsibility for all stakeholders should assume discipline. All should support and agree to the plan. In-service training should be provided if needed. A team approach should be evident in solving problems (Thomas & Walter, 1999).

If implemented, these guidelines will go a long way in promoting support and cooperation from students. As much as possible selected students should be part of the planning and implementation of the plan.

Effective strategic supports are needed for those students who display challenging behaviors resulting from unmet needs. A collaborate team approach is helpful in identifying antecedent strategies such as modification in instructional programs to meet the unique behavioral needs of individuals. Both physical and human resources will be needed to reduce or minimize many behavioral problems. Changes in schedules and the instructional environment may need to be modified to successfully deal with the behavior problems. Other changes and modifications may include alternative skill training, such as social skills, or adaptive skills and long-term preventive strategies. These strategic support structures are primarily designed for those exceptional pupils who constantly break rules on a regular basis.

The State of Pennsylvania (1995) published guidelines for effective behavioral support. The plan was to balance the rights of all students to a safe learning environment while providing effective programs for students with chronic behavioral problems. To achieve this plan, in-service training was provided to the staff and consisted of conducting functional assessment of the behavioral problem. Developing hypotheses relevant to the function of the challenging behavior, designing and implementing the behavioral support plan, evaluating the effectiveness of the plan, and modifying the support plan as needed (Pennsylvania Plan, 1995).

Despite a school-wide discipline plan and positive strategic supports, some individuals within a school building will require a personalized student plan to describe an individualized program of intervention. Guidelines will be needed for behaviors in specific settings other than the classroom. Consistent management practices are needed from classroom to classroom as well as the total school. An essential part of the individualized plan must include a problem-solving process. The process should commence with identifying the target behaviors by conducting a functional assessment to assess the behavior. Next, hypotheses statements should be developed relevant to the target behaviors in order to determine to what degree the stated hypotheses were achieved. The intervention strategies should be developed next, based upon the functional assessment. Using information cited above, an individual plan should be developed and implemented. Documentation of progress and evaluation of the effectiveness of the plan should be carefully assessed., Based upon the evaluative date, the plan may be modified or terminated (Taylor, 2001). An effective plan should include:

1.   Background information on the students.
2.   A succinct description of the problem and an assessment of current performance.
3.   Clearly defined goal statements should be developed.
4.   Well-developed hypotheses statements for the function of the behavior, and intervention strategies related to the function of behavior.
5.   Specific evaluation procedures would be developed before initiating the programs.
6.   Appropriate physical and human resources should be identified before implementing the program. (Jones, 1993; Algozzine, Ruhl, Ramsey, 1991; Breen & Fielder, 1996; Colvin, Kameenui & Sugia, 1993).

Steps in Changing Inappropriate Behaviors

Challenging behaviors are context-related. Behaviors do not occur in a vacuum, individuals select (either consciously, or unconsciously) behaviors in response to their environment (Reavis, Kukic, Jenson, Morgan, Andrews, & Fister, 1996; Sugia, Pruitt, 1993; Walker, Horner, Sugia, Bullis, Sprague, Bricker & Kauffman, 1996).

Challenging behaviors serve a specific function for the student. Although problem behaviors may be socially inappropriate, they are driven by the belief that they will produce a desired result for the student. Student employ many types of challenging behaviors to achieve their goals. Some commonly used behaviors include, obtaining attention, escaping/avoiding a task or demand, obtaining a desired object or activity, satisfying sensory needs, and gaining control of the situation.

These beliefs can be driven by several factors, including past history, observation of others, and a limited repertoire of alternative behaviors. The ultimate goal of student behavior is to fulfill the need to be modified with acceptable alternatives in order to reduce the inappropriate behaviors displayed (Walker, Horner, Sugai, Bullis,

Sprague, Bricker, Kauffman, 1996; Thomas, Grimes, 1995; Mayer, 1995; Colvin 1992; Walker, 1997; Hudley & Graham, 1995).

In implementing the aforementioned steps, all students should be afforded the same dignity and respect, regardless of their differences. Intervention strategies should be designed to assist the child to bring his/her behaviors up to social standards. No intervention should stigmatize, dehumanize, or cause emotional or physical distress to individuals in the program (refer to Appendix A).

A variety of recording instruments must be employed to effectively record and analyze behavioral patterns. In some instances, educators must construct their own recording devices. Refer to Appendices B for an example.

Data received from the instruments may be analyzed to assist educators in determining the effectiveness of their behavioral program. If evaluative results are negative, the student may need additional practice or exposure in behavioral management strategies.

The behavior modifier must address three points, if he/she is to successfully implement a behavior modification strategy: 1) define maladaptive behavior, 2) determine the environmental events which support the behavior, and 3) manipulate the environment in order to alter maladaptive behavior. Thompson and Walter (1999) emphasized that a positive atmosphere should be created in implementing a behavior modification strategy. They proposed that the teacher formulate a positive rule, something students can work toward, rather than something to avoid. By this means, the student is directed toward a specific desirable rather than merely castigated without an alternative suggested behavior. The importance of involving students in planning behavior modification strategy was also outlined (refer to Appendix C).

The teacher should establish a working relationship with each individual. The teacher's job is to assign tasks that the student needs to learn, is ready to learn, and could be successful in learning. This approach permits greater teacher-student interaction. The specific behavior modification strategy, the character of its application, and the nature and quality of the teacher-student interaction must arise out of the teacher's assessment of the individual and his/her needs and interests. A behavior modification strategy should be flexible in its application while firmly based in scientific method (Kaufman, et al., 1998); Colvin, 1992; Mayer, 1995). Due to a wide diversity in mental, physical, and social traits of children, teachers must develop individual behavioral strategies. These strategies must include the aforementioned traits.

The Teacher as a Behavior Modifier

Educators attempt to change the behavior of students in ways which they feel will enhance their desire to learn (refer to Appendix D). Using a behavior modification strategy, educators try to determine those reinforcers which will increase the probability of a desired response or behavior. Several difficulties, however, are inherent in the systematic application of a reinforcer. The first lies in the pupil's perception of his/her current behavior, the target behavior to which he/she is aspiring, and his/her relationship to the reinforcer. By providing an individual with arbitrary reinforcers, a teacher focuses the individual's attention, not on the relationship between his/her behavior and his/her academic or social success, but rather on the relationship between his/her behavior and the reinforcement. He/she sees his/her behavior as related only to the desired consequence and changing his/her behavior has meaning for him/her. The use of natural reinforcers may also be criticized in the same way, although they may more easily be integrated into an individual's frame of reference and thus be more easily related to the desired behavior.

The teacher's attention and praise may function as a negative reinforcer when a teacher utilizes an opportune moment to comment favorably or praise another student in front of the class with the intention of sending a negative message to another student. This type of situation may be called an example of unintended consequences of reinforcement and frequently does not fit the particular life-style of the student. In essence, the method might be harmful to the student unless the teacher has considered his/her individual needs.

Behavior modification is a technique, which may be effectively used in conjunction with educational systems and/or content, it is not a program with content of its own. Generally, teachers feel that the utilization of a behavioral modification strategy is too complex and involves too much preliminary training. These concepts can probably be attributed to the fact that educators are not often familiar with behavioral principles. Teachers who have had adequate training can successfully implement a behavior modification strategy (Taylor, 2001).

Token Reinforcement System

Behavior modification techniques can be highly effective in the beneficial changes of social and academic behaviors of individuals in the classroom or in a school-wide program. Recent research has applied these techniques to preschool children, and to low achieving minority children. The approach that these investigations have taken has been to employ token reinforcers such as colored chips or point cards to improve and maintain improvement of social and/or academic behaviors. Items such as candy, gum, toys, and money have served as back-up reinforcers to these tokens. At some point all tangible reinforcers should be withdrawn and substituted with social reinforcement, when teachers have assessed that tangible reinforcers is no longer need. The process is called extinction.

Extinction

Extinction is associated with eliminating appropriate or inappropriate behaviors through reduction of its reinforcement where negative or positive behavior no longer produces results it gradually fades away. Extinction is a slow process because behavior patterns have become well entrenched. Additionally, when the process is first introduced, the behavior is likely to become worse rather than better because the reinforcers are withdrawn.

Behavior modification is a valuable tool but should not be used as a total approach to classroom learning. Thomas and Grimes (1995), stated that alternative developmental theories might be more helpful for determining goals, support this conviction. These developmental theories may suggest to the teacher a specific developmental task that the student must master and what specific skills the student must acquire in order to achieve subsequent levels of performance.

However, the teacher should be able to recognize the advantages of giving rewards as they relate to a specific goal that is to be obtained. Using this approach, the teacher should be able also to determine when a reward is not working. When the reward becomes the end instead of the means, it becomes a liability. The teacher should become skilled in systematically employing a behavior modification strategy when it will facilitate the acquisition of knowledge and skills designed to make that student a more fully realized individualized in his/her ecological environment and learn how to apply them systematically when difficult discipline problem arise. This necessitates that they employ reinforcement based upon the age and sex of the children.

Summary

Teachers and educational personnel who use behavior modification techniques should make sure that the behavior they choose to change will benefit the student. It is incumbent upon education personnel to be certain their educational goals are moral and ethical. They should have appropriate consequences and a systematic reinforcement system, in order to improve children's behaviors.

The uniqueness of a behavioral strategy lies in its systematic application of a precise technique to bring about behavioral change.

Because of its origin in the scientific laboratory, it requires compliance with and acceptance of the demands of scientific rigor. The development of a behavior modification strategy has established a definite structure whereby a teacher can change a student's behavior. It can be employed to increase the occurrence of desired behavior already within a student's behavioral repertoire or to teach new behavior.

Successful teachers are usually aware of what is most rewarding to their pupils. But many teachers are not aware of the variety of reinforcers available to them in a classroom environment. Many of these various reinforcers are called secondary reinforcers. They are events, which have been frequently paired with primary reinforcers. They are also called conditioned reinforcers.

As was previously noted, a consequence that will reinforce a certain behavior in one child may be ineffective with another. But there are many environmental events which are reinforcing for most pupils, and they can be used to motivate appropriate behaviors. Among these learned or secondary reinforcers are attention, approval, and opportunities to engage in desired behavior or to work with preferred classroom materials. Successful teachers learn what these reinforcers are and they learn how to apply them systematically when difficult discipline problems arise. This requires that the teacher develop her skills in applying reinforcers according to age, sex and reinforcement history. Application of these trait play a crucial role in shaping the behaviors of children.

Consequences that are rewarding for some persons may not be effective as reinforcement for others. Some persons would walk a mile for a cigarette – others would not take one if it was handed to them free. The teacher may see that Glenna beams and works harder if she says, "I'm proud of you!" That same statement may cause Rodney to wince and quit working. Reinforcement must immediately follow the desired behavior.

The more quickly the reinforcement follows the target behavior the more effective it will be. The teacher who comments on how well her pupils are working during the period (while they are actually working) will reinforce them more effectively than the teacher who waits until the end of the day to tell the class how well they studied. (This is especially true if some of the class members did not study very well during the last period of the day.)

Chapter 7

Assertive Discipline

George R. Taylor

Overview

Canter and Canter (1992) wrote that an assertive teacher is "one who clearly and firmly communicates to his/her expectations to his/her students, and is prepared to reinforce his/her words with appropriate actions. He/She responds to students in a manner that maximizes his/her potential to get his/her own needs to teach met, but in no way violates the best interests of the students." The approach is based upon principles employed in behavior modification in that children are rewarded for positive behavior. In assertive discipline, expectations for behaviors are clearly delineated with input from students. Consequences from negative behavior are also clearly defined. When classroom rules are infractioned, students must accept the consequences of their behaviors. Students are taught how to choose responsible and appropriate behaviors in the classroom.

Canter and Canter (1992) firmly believe that factors such as student's emotional problems, inadequate parenting, poverty environment, and do not prohibit children from learning. The major factor which interferes with learning and positive classroom management techniques is a teacher's negative expectations about her ability to deal with disruptive student behavior. Teachers expectations for students' behavior can be too low and praise can be given too frequently.

The Canter Model is designed to assist students to demonstrate self-control and self directed behaviors. Teaching students to assume responsibility for their behavior is an arduous task. One of the major strategies to use in assisting students to assume responsibility for their behavior is the use of language that shift the reason for a behavior to some one else. An example of the negative use of language, "Fred did Mary make you angry?" A positive approach would be to use language that emphasizes personal decisions and responsibility for one's behavior. An example of the positive use of language, "Fred you got really angry with Mary when she took your paper."

Effective use of the model depends how well the teacher understands the development level of the child, individual characteristics, and culture differences. These factors may be responsible for the negative behaviors. Many children with disabilities fit within these categories (Adger, Wolffam, & Detwyler, 1993). Teachers must model and teach children how to act appropriately, once they have defined the mental, social, or physical problem associated with the behavior (Colvin, 1992). Defining and eradicating some of the causes of behaviors are complex and may be beyond the scope of the classroom teacher. In cases of this nature, specialists should be consulted.

Before teachers can effectively change behavior of children the following communication strategies should be employed:

1. Indicate the concise terms that the behavior is unacceptable.
2. Inform the student what is expected.
3. Explore ways to assist the student to improve the unacceptable behavor.
4. Keep communication clear, brief, low key, and as private as possible (Seiler, Schuelke & Lieb-Brilhart, 1984).

The Canter Model is also designed to teach children through a variety of techniques to control their behaviors. Some of the strategies that may be used are physical and social praise, modeling, the use of verbal and non verbal communication skills, including body language, eye contact, facial expressions, direct instruction of expectations and consequences of behavior and reflection of words and voice. Strategies and techniques for using these communication skills will be addressed later in the Chapter.

Discussing inappropriate behaviors with children is a first step in assisting them to take control of their behaviors. The major purpose of discussing inappropriate behavior is to assist children in monitoring, evaluating, and correcting their behaviors (Walker, Colvin & Ramsey, 1995). Students must have standards and expectations set by the teacher and class in order to judge to what extent his/her behavior is inappropriate. Students should receive instruction on how to change his/her behavior and be amenable to changing to more acceptable behavior. Equally important will be the recognition by the student why the change in behavior is necessary (Kameenui & Darch, 1995). Both the teacher and peers should be involved in assisting the student in changing negative behaviors by using some of the aforementioned strategies (Utley, Mortweet & Greenwood, 1987). Additionally, the Canter Model emphasizes how teachers can deal effectively with aggressive and hostile behaviors.

Types of Response Styles

The way teachers respond to students will significantly set the tone in the classroom. The tone effects how student feel about themselves and the teacher. Response styles are classified as nonassertive, hostile and assertive.*

A non assertive style may described as when the teacher is passive in responding to student behavior. Teachers employing this style do not communicate his/her expectations to follow and may become confused by not knowing what to expect or how a teacher may respond to a certain behavior.

A hostile response style is characterized by a teacher who is rigid, authoriatarian, iron-fisted, and inflexible. These strategies are employed by teachers to control students rather than to teach them to control their own behavior. Hostile responses debase the self-esteem of children, diminish self-confidence, and impact upon positive child and teacher relationships. Frequently, teachers use this style because they believe it is the only way to get students to behave appropriately (Canter & Canter, 1992).

An assertive response style is characterized by the teacher clearly articulating and consistently stating his/her expectations to students, and a plan to reinforce expectations with actions. Assertive responses imply that a teacher clearly communicates to student which behaviors are acceptable and which ones are not acceptable, and the consequences for choosing either type of behavior. Teachers using assertive response style know the limits of his/her students and set expectations within these limits. Also, teachers using this technique teach children how to correct their behavior. The teacher communicates his/her response in a firm but polite way to students. This response sends a direct and clear message of

---

* For specific examples of response types refer to Lee Canter and Marlene Canter (1992). Assertive Discipline. Santa Monica, CA: Lee Canter and Associates.

the behavior the teacher expects. It is recommended over the two other approaches in controlling behavior. A class discipline plan is an essential part of assertive disciplines, where students and all stakeholders participate in its development. It should make managing student behavior easier, project students might and assist in ensuring parental and administrative support (Kerr & Nelson, 1998).

A Classroom Discipline Plan

An effective assertive discipline program requires a well developed plan designed to teach children to choose responsible behavior (Rhode, Jenson, & Reavis, 1992). The plan should permit teachers to clarify the behaviors expected from students and what students can expect from teachers in return. It should promote a fair and systematical way to develop a safe and orderly classroom. The plan should be flexible enough to allow teachers to infuse behavior management into the instructional program. Canter and Canter (1992) listed three components that should be included in a discipline plan. They are rules, positive recognition, and consequences.

Rules

Rules should be kept to a minimum and be general and simple enough to apply to any circumstances in the classroom. They should be observable and designed to teach appropriate classroom behavior. When possible children should be included in developing rules. The needs and maturity of the children should be considered when developing rules. Teacher should make sure that rules are appropriate for the age levels of children. Some simple rules which appear to cut across all grade levels include: 1) follow directions, 2) respect others, no profanity or teasing, 3) keep hands, feet and objects to yourself, and 4) speak softly. As indicated, rules may have to be taught to some children (Taylor, 1998).

Positive Recognition

In order to bring about effective behavioral changes in children, teachers must motivate children to demonstrate appropriate behavior in the classroom. It requires that a teacher and children develop realistic behavioral expectations for children to achieve. When teachers use positive recognition the following benefits are achieved (Kerr & Nelson, 1998):
1)   Increased self-esteem of students;
2)   Continued appropriate behaviors;
3)   Reduced problem behaviors;
4)   Improved relationship between children and teachers.
Praise is the most effective positive recognition teachers can give children. Positive recognition of children's behavior can also be promoted through

positive notes, and telephone calls to parents and giving children awards and special privileges for demonstrating appropriate behaviors.

Consequences

In effect, a discipline plan must have consequences built in for inappropriate behaviors. Children, parents, and other related individuals should be involved in developing the consequences. Children must become acutely aware that inappropriate behaviors necessitate consequences. Teachers should constantly remind children of the consequences for inappropriate behavior.

Children should be given a choice whether they prefer to deter the inappropriate behavior or choose the consequence. The nature and extent of the inappropriate behavior should match the consequence given. Consequences do not have to be severe in order to be effective. Moreover, all consequences do not have to be the same, but gradually increase based upon the number and extent of time a student performs an inappropriate act (Macht, 1990).

In some cases of severe types of inappropriate behaviors that disrupt the classroom, a student should lose his/her right to choose consequences. Students falling in this group should be immediately removed from the classroom.

Teachers need to develop a system to record student inappropriate behaviors and the consequences imposed. Canter and Canter (1992) maintain that each student must start each day with a clean slate, consequences should not accumulate from day to day. The authors list the following consequences that teachers may used in their classroom:

1. Time out – removing a student from the group;
2. One-minute wait after class;
3. Written assignment in behavioral journal;
4. Detention;
5. Loss of a special privilege;
6. Last to leave class.

Teaching the Discipline Plan

Once all the aforementioned components of the discipline plan have been developed, the next step is to teach the plan to children. All major components should be taught beginning with clarifying the rules, consequences, and positive recognition as soon as the plan is completed. Equally important to the success of the plan will be student understanding of their expectations of the various components of the plan. Children in the lower elementary grades and some children with disabilities may require additional teaching time than students in the upper grades (Canter & Canter, 1992).

Teaching Responsible Behavior

Children must be taught how to make responsible behavioral choices in the classroom and in school. Directions for making appropriate choices and routine procedures should be well articulated to children. Teachers should teach directions for completing selected activities, such as directed lessons in front of the class, independent seat work, cooperative learning group, group discussions, taking a test, working at learning centers. Routine procedures include general classroom activities which usually include students moving to complete an activity or to satisfy a need (Taylor, 1999; Kauffman, Mostert, & Hallahan, 1998). The development of and age levels of children must be taken in consideration when teaching directions. Young children and those with disabilities will require additional instructional time.

Implementing the Plan

Positive recognition should be infused with teaching responsible behavior. Teachers should reinforce students who follow directions and positively remind students who are not following direction in a calm and understanding manner. Other suggested strategies teachers may employ using positive recognition:

1.   Take time to infuse consistent praise into an activity;
2.   Use scanning techniques in the classroom to identify inappropriate behaviors;
3.   Circulate through out the classroom give praise when appropriate;
4.   Recognize good behavior by writing names on board;
5.   Use positive support to increase students' self-esteem;
6.   Use positive support to reduce behavior problems;
7.   Attempt to praise every student every day;
8.   Use positive recognition to motivate children to work toward a special behavioral goal.

A well developed management plan will address most classroom behavior problems, however there are two types of behaviors which should be included, one of which may be over looked by the teacher. These behaviors are referred to as disruptive off-task behavior and on-disruptive off-task behavior. Disruptive off-task behaviors are easily recognized because they interfere with the learning process of the classroom. Specific rules and expectations can be developed in the play to address these behaviors. On the other hand, teachers may over look non-disruptive off-task behaviors since they do not usually impact learning in the classroom, only the individual student, such behaviors as day dreaming, looking out of the window or other behaviors which draw a student from the instructional task. These behaviors impede the student's learning and teachers should immediately employ the consequence for the behavior with care and understanding in order to direct the student back on tasks (Alberto & Troutman, 1995).

There are several strategies that teacher may use to redirect students back on task. Sometimes a frequent look, signifying disapproval is sufficient. Other techniques include physical proximity, call a students name while teaching, and proximity praise, praising students around the student showing inappropriate behavior.

Using Consequences Effectively

Many types of disciplinary problem can be addressed through the use of consequences to assist student in choosing appropriate behaviors. Canter and Canter (1992) have provided the following guidelines for using consequences:

1. Provide consequences in a calm, matter-of-fact manner;
2. Be consistent. Provide a consequence every time a student choose to disrupt;
3. After a student receives a consequence, find the first opportunity you can to recognize positive behavior;
4. Provide an "escape mechanism" for students who are upset and want to talk about what happened;
5. "Move in" when a student continuously disrupts.

In some instances teachers may need to dispense with the stated guidelines and use their own judgment by not using consequences when students are extremely upset and crying. Providing a consequence would do little to control the behavior. Times like these the teacher must consider what is best for the child and use his/her best judgment.

Problem Solving Conference

Some students' behaviors are so disruptive until traditional approaches, such as discipline plans may not be sufficient. Teachers may have to resort to problem solving conferences. Professional services beyond the scope of the teacher and school may be needed (Anderson & Decker, 1993). Most cases, however, are not severe enough to seek professional services beyond the classroom. When teachers set up a one-to-one conference with students some basic principles should be considered. Let the student know that your are genuinely concerned about him/her as an individual and that you have his best interest at heart. Pose questions which do not constitute threat to the student's self-image. Attempt to draw from the student the underlying reasons for the behavior. Offer your support and suggestions for improving the situation. Encourage the students to give his/her own solution to the problem. The teacher should consider the student's input and collectively come up with an action plan. The action plan should include the teacher's expectations needed to change the behavior. Key points reached should be summarized and agreed upon on how the student can demonstrate more responsible behavior .

Summary

Assertive discipline has proven to be an effective technique for controlling inappropriate behaviors. Teachers require no special training for implementing the model. Principles of behavior modification can easily be seen in the model. All stakeholder involved with the child, as well as the child himself, should be involved in the development, implementation and evaluation of the plan. The plan should be taught to the children and they must fully be apprised of all components.

Reflexibility in assertive discipline enable teachers to adapt the model to suit the individual needs of students in his/her classroom. The model also permits teachers to incorporate other classroom management theories and models in their Assertive Discipline Plan.

Chapter 8

Dreikurs Conceputal Model

George R. Taylor

Overview

Dreikurs Model is based upon the premise that most student misbehavior is a result of the need to belong or not feeling worthwhile. When those traits are negative they influenced why student misbehave. Dreikurs (1968) categorized misbehavior into the following types: 1) attention getting, 2) power seeking, 3) revenge seeking, and 4) displays of inadequacy. These behaviors displayed by students require a different response by the teacher. In some instances Dreikurs recommends that the teacher should not become involved in the incident. Once teachers understand the behavioral patterns of his/her students they may appeal to logical reasoning for some students to self-correct their behaviors. The importance of student involvement in developing rules are essential to the model. A word of caution is in order for teachers desiring to use this model, extensive training is needed to implement the model successfully.

Logical reasoning implies that children are given a choice rather than being directed by the teacher to change a behavior. Children must internalize the consequences of their behavior and act accordingly (Kerr & Nelson, 1998; Walker, 1995). In logical consequences, the teacher anticipates how the student will respond. Example: A student was constantly walking out of line. This was in violation of one of the class rules. The teacher asked the student if he preferred to walk behind the class or with the class. The student said that he would prefer to walk behind the class. The teacher explained to the student and class that he would no longer have his position in the line. The student moved to the rear of the line. After several days, the teacher asked whether or not the student preferred to walk behind the line or take his position in the line. He said that he preferred to take his position in the line. The student no longer walked out of line.

According to Dreikurs (1960), behavior is driven by an individual's purposes, even behavior that is destructive is purposeful because each behavior is self-determined and self-directed. Children frequently behave based upon their concepts of what is appropriate or inappropriate as well as models they have seen in their environments. They may not realize that their inappropriate perception may lead them to be rejected by their peers or to engage in behaviors which are deemed inappropriate in the classroom. Teachers should employ strategies as outlined in the above examples to assist students in making logical choices concerning their behaviors.

Causes of Inappropriate Behavior

In Chapter 1, we summarized some of the social/environmental causes of behavior. The psychological dimensions are equally as important when these dimensions are not satisfied. Children usually misbehave to achieve them. Dreikurs (1968) has identified four schemes that children employ to achieve their goals 1) gaining attention, 2) exercising powerful, 3) exacting revenge, and 4) displaying inadequacy. In achieving goals, children usually follow schemes as outlined. They do not achieve success with the first scheme, they continue until they find the scheme which will give them attention.

Gaining Attention

This aspect is considered to be the first step used by children to draw attention to themselves. These behaviors are a source of distraction in the classroom and may manifest themselves by children being disruptive, not completing assignments, crying and refusing to complete work. The attention getting strategies only appear to work when they have the teacher's approval. Edwards (1997) contended that giving attention to attention-seeking children does not necessarily improve their behavior. When attention is given in response to children's misbehavior, the misbehavior increases. Teaching strategies should be designed to reduce attention-seeking behaviors through using the following patters: 1) active-constructive, 2) passive-constructive, 3) active-destructive, and 4) passive-destructive (Dreikurs, Grunwold, & Pepper, 1992; Dreikurs, Bronia, & Pepper, 1998).

Active-Constructive Behavior. The authors classified active-constructive children as cooperative and conform to expectations. These children are usually programmed for success according to adult standards however, they relate very poorly to their peers. The authors listed other traits of these children as being:

1)   very competitive;
2)   attempt to maintain superiority over others;
3)   role models for the teacher;
4)   tattler on others;
5)   unable to tolerate being ignored.

These children are highly ambitious and will do most anything with adult expectations, to meet the teacher's praise and recognition. Teachers should attempt to ignore unacceptable behavior. Recognition of their behaviors reinforce them. If behaviors are ignored, children will learn to associate attention with inappropriate behavior (Dreikurs, 1968; Fulk, 1997).

Passive-Constructive Behavior. These children attempt to receive attention through passive behaviors such as charming and manipulating other, including adults, into meeting their demands. They flatter others and have close relations with those that they depend upon. Their behaviors are never involved in destructive behaviors, but use the power of persuasion to achieve their goals.

Active-Destructive Behavior. Children who demonstrate these behaviors are defiant, clownish, bullying and impertinent. They are usually persistent in achieving their goals and will stop at nothing until they receive attention, when attention is achieved the behaviors dissipate.

Passive-Destructive Behavior. Children showing this behavior are characterized as lazy. Through negative action they force their peers to feel sorry for them and want to be assured by them. They pretend that they do not understand or the assignments are too difficult. Behaviors in this pattern include bashfulness, dependency, untidiness, lack of concentration, and self-indulgence.

Exercising Power

When some children cannot have their way or gain the attention of parents and teachers, they resort to a power struggle. It is difficult for teachers to restrain themselves when children make a play for power. When teachers and parents attempt to control the behavior of these children, it only increases their determination and anxiety levels, thus, increasing power-seeking behaviors. Teachers by and large are unprepared to avoid power struggles with students who threaten their authority. Types of power seeking behavior include throwing temper tantrums, lying, crying, being stubborn and disobedient. Many teachers and parents are sympathetic toward children showing these behaviors. Power seeking children take advantage of sympathetic adults who try to control them by demonstrating the above behaviors. The problem becomes critical when power seeking children behaviors influence the class attitudes toward the teacher. In some instances the teacher may need to develop group strategies to deal with the problem. Teacher may present he problem to the class or have the power-seeking student present the problem and have the class to make decisions. Teachers should remember not to fight with students. Power struggles can frequently be avoided if the teacher just ignores the behavior (Kauffman, Lloyd, & McGee, 1989; Kauffman, 1997).

Exacting Revenge

Interventions by teachers to control some children's behavior are viewed by some children as unfair. They view this action as a planned intent to hurt them. These children attempt to take out their revenge on anyone near them. They manifest revenge by destroying their own property, property of others, kicking, tripping, hitting, knocking objects on the floor and other destructive acts. Destructive acts may also be directed toward the teacher such as marking the teacher's desk, destroying objects on the teacher's desks, placing objects in the teacher's chair, defacing personal property of the teacher, publicly defying the teacher and tearing pages from books. Teachers can seek class members to assist them in having the class being more tolerant toward them. They may need mental health specialists to assist them in reducing destructive behaviors of those children because many are not aware of the hostility they create (Walker, 1995; Kerr & Nelson, 1998).

Displaying Inadequacy

Children who do not achieve a degree of self worth through the aforementioned types of behaviors may develop a low concept of themselves and withdraw from classroom and group activities. The little self-esteem they have left is used avoiding any type of group activity. They believe that this approach will make other children leave them alone if they are thought to be socially inadequate. These children hope that their inadequately will draw attention to them and that they will be accepted. Behaviors displayed by these children include being: 1) overly ambitious, 2) overly competitive, and 3) overly sensitive. Teachers should develop techniques and strategies to encourage the child to feel positive about himself/herself. They should also assist the class in accepting the inadequacy of the child (Kameenui & Darch, 1995; Walker, Colvin & Ramsey, 1995).

Assisting Children in Correcting Their Misbehaviors

Before misbehaviors of children can be corrected, teachers must provide strategies to assist them in internalizing their misbehaviors. They must bring them to the conscious level and recognize what they are doing as well as recognizing the impact that their misbehaviors have upon others. To assist teachers in helping students correct their misbehaviors Dinkmeyer and Dinkmeyer (1976) listed several steps to assist them in using logical consequences. These suggestions are very broad in scope, leaving teachers to be creative and innovative in using them. However, before these approaches are successful, teacher must establish a good rapport with children. The steps suggested are:

1. Teachers attempt to ascertain students' motives;
2. Students are helped to understand their motives;
3. Students are helped to exchange their mistaken goal for useful ones;
4. Students are encouraged to become committed to their new goal orientation;
5. Students are taught to apply logical consequences; and
6. Group discussions regarding class rules and problems are held.

Understanding Misbehaving Students

Inappropriate behaviors do not occur in a vacuum. There are social/environmental reasons which precipitate behaviors, as indicated in Chapter 1. In addition, teachers must become cognizant of psychological reasons for misbehaving, as well as having a knowledge of principles of child growth and development (Alberto & Troutman, 1995; Kauffman, 1997). Without these factors it is doubtful whether or not teachers can assist students in recognizing, altering or changing their goals and behaviors. Due to a variety of factors such as developmental, environmental, social, and poor role models, many children do not fully understand why they behave as they do. When teacher assist them in understanding their goals and motives, misbehaving behaviors are significantly reduced. Dreikurs, Grunwald & Pepper (1982)* proposed that teachers pose the following questions to assist children to reveal their goals and motives.

1. Do you know why you _____? (Even if a child does not know the reason for the misbehavior, this question is raised in preparation for the next step.)
Would you like for me to tell you what I think? (Question from "Gaining Attention", "Exercising Power", Exacting Revenge", and "Displaying Inadequacy", as related to the goals and motives

of the children one asked. Dreikurs, Grunwald & Pepper (1982) have developed a list of questions under the listed categories that teachers may use. The authors recommend that when a student answer is "no" to a teachers initial question, following questions should be posed until the child's answer is "maybe", or "perhaps". Charles (1992) reports that from children responses, the teacher should be able to analyze how the child feels. The teacher can also observe the behaviors and actions of students to assist them in identifying inappropriate goals and behaviors.

Uses of Logical Consequences in the Classroom

Before attempting using logical consequences in the classroom teachers should be aware of the advantages and disadvantages of using the model and identify logical consequences in advance of employing them (Dreikurs, Grunwald, & Pepper, 1982, 1998; Dreikurs, Bronia, & Pepper, 1998).

Advantages

There are several advantages for teachers using this model. It assists children in recognizing, identifying and correcting misbehaviors, thus decreasing discipline problems in the classroom. Strategies and techniques are developed to assist children in understanding how they behave as they do and provide assistance for them to minimize, correct, or reduce maladaptive behavior. The strategies and techniques employed are designed to assist children in recognizing and internalizing their behaviors. No significant changes can occur in behaviors before children learn to bring problems to the conscious level. The model assists in bonding teachers and children by promoting mutual respect between them. Discipline problems are corrected through the use of logical sequences rather than punishment and rewards. It also assists teachers in focusing on the causes of behaviors before corrective measures are taken (Dreikurs, Bronia, & Pepper, 1998).

Disadvantages

The disadvantages of the model are few. Since teachers are not trained mental health specialists they may have some difficulty determining the goals and motives of the children. There is no way of determining whether or not students are revealing their true motives, either because they believe that their motives will not be accepted or they

---

*   R. Dreikurs, RB.B. Grunwald, & F.C. Pepper (1982). Maintaining sanity in the classroom: Classroom Management Techniques (2nd ed.) New York: Harper & Row.

do not know how to identify them. Teachers may find it difficult to respond to students non authoritative way as well as the in-depth involvement of engaging in conversation with student (Dreikurs, Bronia, & Pepper, 1998).

Summary

A word of caution is in order when using logical consequences. Sometimes teachers relate the concept with punishment. Punishment, according to Dreikurs & Cassel (1972) promotes revenge and causes students to feel that they have a right to retaliate. Students do not associate punishment with their own behavior but rather with the person providing it. Punishment does not teach children how to correct their behavior, but encourages more inappropriate behavior. Logical consequences, when understood by students, are more readily accepted by students because they help to determine the consequences, and it teaches children ways of correcting their behaviors. Demonstrate principles are essential to the model.

Dreikurs Model (1982) list some recommendations for an effective discipline model. The list is divided between some do's and don'ts.

Some Do's

1. Always try first to understand the purpose of children's misbehavior.
2. Give clear-cut directions for actions expected of children.
3. Focus on children's present, not their past, behavior.
4. When children misbehave in class, give them a choice either to remain where they are without disturbing others or to leave the room.
5. Build on the positive and avoid the negative.
6. Build trust between yourself and children.
7. Discuss children's behavior problems only when neither you nor they are emotionally charged.
8. Use logical consequences instead of punishment.
9. Treat children with consistency.
10. Use cooperative planning to establish goals and solutions to problems.
11. own Let children assume increasingly greater responsibility for their behavior and learning as they are able to do so.
12. Use the whole class to create and enforce rules.
13. Be kind but firm with children.
14. Show that you accept children but not their misbehavior.

15.   Help children become more responsibly independent.
16.   Make sure that students understand the limits.

Some Don'ts

1.   Do not be preoccupied with your own prestige and authority.
2.   Refrain from nagging and scolding which may reinforce misbehaving children's quest for attention.
3.   Do not ask children to promise anything. They will make a promise to get out of an uncomfortable situation with no intention of fulfilling it.
4.   Avoid giving rewards for good behavior. Doing so will only condition children to expect rewards.
5.   Refrain from finding fault with children.
6.   Do not hold your students and yourself to different standards.
7.   Do not use threats.
8.   Do not be vindictive.
9.   Do not ignore or tolerate misbehaviors. If ignored, inappropriate behaviors may lead to serious problems and will become in the absence of intervention.

Chapter 9

Thomas Gordon Model

George R. Taylor

Overview

Teacher effectiveness training has a long and productive record for training teacher's school personnel and parents how to avoid discipline problems. According to Gordon (1989) and Taylor (1977) this model is an alternative to punishment. Research has shown that punishment of all kinds increase the incidence of misbehavior rather than reduce it. Additionally, research findings have shown that punishment impedes the development of effective discipline of children (Straus, Gelles, & Steinmetz, 1980). In support of the cited research, Gordon (1989) wrote that children who have been coerced usually show poor self-control one they are outside of the influence of adult's controllers. Punishment will not prevent children's aggressive behavior, instead it actually causes aggression in children. According to Kauffman, Mostert, Trent & Hallahan (1998) punishment may take two forms, by either withdrawing what the children desire or by instituting unpleasant or negative consequences. All punishment does not cause serious physical and psychological pain. Punishment may cause some physical or psychological stress but should not produce stress within children. The most effective type of punishment involves using a consequence that decreases the reoccurrence of the behavior, such as withdrawing the positive reinforce associated with the behavior.

Guidelines, for using punishment effectively. The following guidelines are recommended before teachers use punishment.

1.   Use positive consequences to reduce inappropriate behavior.

2.   Reward children consistently for displaying positive behaviors.

3.   Administer punishment as a last resort without anger or threats.

4.   Administer punishment as a last resort equally and consistently to all children.

5.   Can behavioral changes be seen as a result of punishment?

6.   Are the consequences of punishment understood by stakeholders concerned, including administrators, parents, and children?

7.   Reduce the use of punishment through teaching appropriate social skills.

8.   Make sure that the instructional program does not attribute to inappropriate behavior which may result in using punishment.

The listed guidelines should be administered with input from children relevant to the individual needs and learning styles. Educators should consider the guidelines when administering punishment to children.

Using Power-Based Control

Adult controllers frequently employ power-based control to regulate the behaviors of children during childhood. When children enter adolescence, adult controllers loose their power. This is chiefly due to local and state laws concerning punishment to correct inappropriate behavior. They usually resort to ineffective punishments such as making children write excessive statement relevant to their behaviors, staying after school, sending to the principal office and missing recess are to name but a few (Friedman, 1999).

Adult controllers who employ power-based discipline with children force them to develop coping behaviors. Gordon (1989) has listed 24 of these behavior including rebelling, counter attacking, defying vandalizing, breaking rules, throwing temper tantrums, lying, blaming others, showing hostile behaviors, bossing others, carrying favors with adults, withdrawing behaviors, competing, immature behavior, developing physical and psychological ailments and using drugs. These coping behaviors are skillfully employed by children to make it uncomfortable for adults who attempt to control their behavior.

Concerning the issue of using rewards, Gordon's views are that teachers use rewards to control children by making them dependent upon the reward. Teachers can exercise control over students as long as students are kept in a constant state of dependency. Grading is commonly used in school as a reward. Grading work fair for high achieving children but offer little incentive for low achieving children. In order to receive high grades, as well as most reward which have significant interests, children may resort to all types of inappropriate behaviors to receive them, such as cheating, stealing, and copying. Praise is also used by teachers. As a reward children often seek praise from teachers by attempting to please them. Teachers employ praise to motivate children to complete assigned tasks and other academic work. Teachers should use praise with caution by making sure that a certain standard or behavior is necessary to achieve praise.

Effectiveness of Training

Gordon (1989) strongly educated against the use of rewards and punishment as effective ways of controlling the behavior of children. This view is in contrast to models, such as Behavior Modification and Assertive Discipline, in which rewards are essential components. Gordon's major criticism to the behavioral model is that it attempts to control children rather than give them choices. Giving children choices imply teachers and educators to reframe from using resistance, rebellion, and blaming tactics instead of strategies which promotes self-confidence and self-regulation strategies. Children's views of inappropriate behaviors may differ from the teacher's perception. Basically, children's behaviors are designed to achieve their needs. The conflict between teachers and children arise when the achievement of needs are perceived differently. Teachers should be more tolerant, and understanding of motives which drive children to satisfy their needs and attempt to provide alternative strategies to assist them.

Who Owns the Problem?

Teachers should ascertain who owns the problem. They sometime attempt to force changes in problems owned by the student. When this occurs, communication is impeded in assisting students in solving their problems. Gordon (1989) considers the following strategies unaccepted in trying to solve students' problems: 1) ordering, commanding and directing; 2) warning, and threating; 3) moralizing, preaching, "shoulds and oughts", 4) advising, offering, solutions, or suggestions; 5) teaching, lecturing, giving logical arguments; 6) judging, criticizing, disagreeing, blaming; 7) stereo-typing, labeling; 8) interpreting, analyzing, diagnosing; 9) praising, agreeing, giving positive evaluations; 10) reassuring, sympathizing, consoling, supporting; 11) questioning, probing, interrogating, cross-examining, and 12) withdrawing, distracting, being sarcastic.

The listed roadblocks generally communicate unacceptance to students, basically because the roadblocks indicate that childrens' behaviors are inappropriate. Gordon stated that sometimes teachers send indirect messages to students in an effort to solve problems that they create. These messages may be kidding and teasing or sarcasm. Additionally, when students display inappropriate behaviors, mostly all teachers send confrontational messages to students. Students respond to these messages by resistances, guilt, or shame with a desire to defend themselves. These messages do little to help in solving problems. Teachers need to develop strategies to assess and identify why the behaviors occurred and provide alternate ways to solve the problem. Gordon recommends that teachers accept students' behavior attempts to justify their needs instead of inappropriate behavior by making inquiries to clarify the behavior.

Teachers may also employ the pre-mask principle in solving problems. This principle involves substituting an unacceptable behavior for one that is acceptable. The effects of the classroom environment of behavior must be considered by teachers. A classroom which over or under stimulates learning may cause children to react inappropriately in order to satisfy their needs. Children become easily distracted when their interests are not addressed in the classroom. They also may become bored when their individual needs are not properly addressed. Effective teachers should provide a variety of learning activities to reduce inappropriate behaviors in the classroom. Frequently, teachers should make changes in the physical and psychological environment in order to enhance students' learning Taylor, 1998).

Listening Activities

Many teachers have not learned to listen attentively to children. Listening to children can be very effective in having them to analyze and solve their problems. Additionally, a teacher who listens attentively conveys to the student that he/she is willing to assist and support the student. Gordon (1974) related when students indicate that their feelings have been understood and accepted it is considered a supportive response. Teachers should access and use the best listening strategy they think will assist the child. Passive listening has proven to be a successful strategy to employ as well as verbal and non-verbal clues. Gordon (1989) listed door openers as an effective technique, where teachers pose direct questions with no evaluative content. The technique is designed to promote better communication and to assist to explore their problems. Teacher's silence may also be used to improve communication between teacher and student. Active listening promotes children to reveal the true causes of their problems.

Initially, when students first attempt to communicate their true feelings, they are not completely showing their true feelings. Children usually make guarded statements relevant to their feelings until a sense of trust has been established in the person they are communicating. When children gain confidence in teachers and other significant adults, much progress can be made in assisting them in solving their problems. Gordon (1974) has summed up traits which teachers may employ to be effective listeners: 1) a deep sense of trust in students to solve their own problems; 2) genuinely accept the feeling expressed by students; 3) under that feelings are transitory; 4) want to help students with their problems; 5) show empathy; 6) improve communication through actively listening; and 7) respect the privacy and confidentially of students' problems.

Confronting I-Messages

When behaviors such as boisterous, stubborn, loud, aggressive, hostile, annoying, and selfish are demonstrated by children, active listening strategies are not recommended. The following may be problems owned by the teacher. Instead confronting I- Messages from teachers are necessary. Gordon (1974) contended that when students own problems, teachers take a role of being active listeners, are primarily interested in the students' needs, and are more passive in problem solving. When teachers own problems, they send messages to their students mostly to satisfy their own needs, and take an active part in problem solving. Three variables are necessary for teaches to work with in changing inappropriate behaviors, the student, the environment, and teachers themselves. Modifying student's behaviors may include many strategies induced by the teacher, such as giving directives. The environment may be modified by moving rearranging seating and groups. Teachers may modify their behaviors by given student more time on task to complete assignments.

Gordon (1974) recommended that teachers need to determine problem ownership and then send I-Messages that address problems and their ownership sending I-Messages involve communicating what is creating a problem for the teacher, non-blaming, and non-judgmental description of what the teacher finds unacceptable. I-Messages, according to Gordon, should begin with "when". This conveys to students that it is just at particular times their specific behaviors are a problem and that there are strategies students can employ to change their behavior. I-Messages also reflect the tangible or concrete effect the specific behavior has on the teacher. Finally, I-messages are a statement of the feelings generated within teachers by their students. When teachers use the three components discussed relative to I-Messages, they influence students to change and show that teachers are human and have some of the same wants and needs as they have. When teaches receive resistance to I-Messages, they should shift to listening strategies shifting to listening frequently reduce students' resistance.

Problem Solving Techniques

Sometimes problems displayed by children cannot be effectively resolved through I-Messages or shifting gears. Teachers may have to use problem solving techniques and employ the following steps: 1) define the problem; 2) generate possible solutions; 3) evaluate each solution; 4) make a decision; 5) determine how to implement the decision, and 6) access the success of the decision (Gordon, 1974). When defining problems Gordon stated that it is appropriate for teachers to provide I-Messages so that students will know exactly how they feel. Teachers should also practice active listening so that students will be prompted to provide accurate descriptions of the needs. Both teachers and students should offer solutions to the problem. These solutions should be evaluated with input from children. Solutions receiving a prepondence of negative responses should be dropped from the list. All children should accept the solution or agree to try it and evaluate its effectiveness. Solutions which receive negative ratings should be dropped and new solutions developed to address the problem.

Student conflict which involves value conflicts seldom can be addressed using the aforementioned strategies. Within this framework, students do not normally see a problem with their behavior. When dealing with value laden conflicts teacher must gain the acceptance of the group. Students will only trust teachers and school officials when they believe that their values are not being evaluated, and they are willing to discuss their values. The responsibility of changing values should be left up to the student. Teachers should serve as consultants and provide new information about new ways of thinking, and mode what they value. Gordon (1974) reflected that modeling couldn't be expected to automatically alter student values. However, teachers who honestly model their values will earn the respect and trust of the students.

Prevention of Problems

Gordon's teacher effectiveness training program does little to provide strategies for preventing inappropriate behaviors. This model suggests that teachers conduct open-ended classroom discussions concerning the problem. During this forum children should be given opportunities to offer solutions to the problem. Gordon (1989) indicated that "preventive I-Messages" are designed to get students to modify unaccepted behaviors which have already occurred, and designed to modify future student behaviors. Students are apprised ahead of time what teachers expect. To be effective in using this model, teacher should not sound aggressive or demanding.

Summary

According to Gordon (1989, 1974) the "Teacher-Effectiveness Training Model" is designed to promote autonomy and self-regulation for students. This autonomy promotes good student-teacher relationship by improving communication by assisting students in recognizing that teachers have feelings and allows students to recognize and evaluate their problems. The model denounces the use controlling student behavior through reward and punishment. Road blocks to effective communication, such as ordering, threatening, preaching, and criticizing, have no place in the model. The importance of teachers effectively using I-Messages to assist children in changing their behaviors is an essential part of the model. Some teachers may find changing their roles from directing and controlling to active learning and problem solving, as well as accepting value differences between themselves and their students.

Chapter 10

The Jones Model

George R. Taylor

Overview

The Jones Model is based on a low teacher profile in keeping students on task and controlling events which may lead to disruptive behavior in the classroom. According to Jones (1987a) the Model contains the following:

1.   Classroom management procedures must be positive and promote cooperation. The classroom atmosphere should be free of coercion and punishment.

2.   Discipline standards and procedures must be practical, simple and well understood by students. Teachers should make sure that all students understand the procedures. In some instances the procedures may have to modeled.

3.   Procedures in the model should reduce the teachers workload. The teacher is freer to develop his/her instructional program rather than focusing on distributive behaviors.

4.   The classroom should be properly structured. The physical environment should be conducive to learning. Seating arrangements should permit freedom of movement for both teacher and students seating arrangement should not hinder access to students.

5.   Strategies for enabling the teacher to establish control in the classroom through the use of appropriate instructional strategies. The instructional program is designed to reduce behavior problems by individualizing instruction as much as possible.

6.   Cooperation between the teacher, children, and parents are essential to the success of the model. All must understand roles and functions and work as a team.
7.   Develop an appropriate backup system. The strategies and procedures in the model may be infused with other models presented. The teacher may also use other human resources in the school such as the counselor, social worker and the psychologist for assistance.

Classroom Structures (Mato and Topic)
Rules, Routines and Standards

Jones (1987a) firmly believes that make sure that students fully understand rules, routines, and standards will enhance classroom management and significantly reduce behavior problems. He lists several misconceptions that teachers should be aware:

1.   Students already know how to behave when they reach your class.
2.   Teachers should avoid spending too much time going over the rules because doing so takes two much time from the instructional program.
3.   Rules are general guidelines.
4.   Announcing the rules of the class will ensure that they all understood.
5.   If you do a good job teaching your rules at the beginning of the school year, you will not have to refer to them again.
6.   Discipline is essentially a motion of strictly enforcing the rules.
7.   Student inherently dislikes and resent classroom rules.

In order to avoid the misconceptions listed, teachers should teach rules, routines and standards on a regular basis as they would teach academic subjects. Students need rules and procedures clarified, if not they will set their own limits. They should understand and be able to follow the rules and routines as standards. Teachers should seek the support of students for rules and procedures, through group discussions. Rules should be democratically developed with input from students. Most students appreciate an organized, and tranquil classroom and appreciate a firm, but fair teacher (Jones & Jones, 1989, 2000).

As with most discipline models discussed in the text, seating arrangements are of prime importances, the same principle holds true for the Jone's Model. In this Model classroom furniture is arranged to permit teachers to have greater mobility and access to students. The fewer the physical barriers between the teacher and students the greater is accessibility. The teacher's desk should be placed in a position so that it does not restrict her/his movement. Placing the teachers' desk in the front of the room may restrict movement. Ideally, students' desk should be close to the chalkboard. In some classrooms teachers assign desk to students based upon selected criteria, such as set, achievement, alphabetically or randomly. In other cases teachers permit students to choose their own seats. High achieving students tend to be seated near the front of the room. Disruptive students lend to be seated in the back of the room. To avoid this type of arrangement, intervention is needed by the teacher to mix and alter the seating arrangement for high achievers and disruptive students. Student should be apprised that the seating arrangement is not permanent, and subject to changes periodically.

Jones suggest that seating arrangement provide enough space for the teacher to be mobile and permit enough room for independent and group activities. According to Jones' accessible seating arrangements, all seats and desks should face the chalkboard, and the arrange patterns of the desk would differ as shown in Figure 10.1. Teachers should experiment with various types of seating arrangements, but this model requires that the chalkboard is at the front of the room.

Rapport Between Teacher and Children

Establishing rapport is an important and essential test that teachers must develop. Children need to know that they are like and respected by the teacher. They also want to know that the teacher will respect, if not always agree with, their opinions. When rapport is well established, and a sense of trust prevails in the classroom, learning is accelerated. In this positive environment children are encouraged to make their own decisions without punitive reaction from the teacher. If the teacher sets a positive tone in the classroom, and teaches children to make appropriate choices, most children can become self-directed (Taylor, 1997).

Figure 10.1
Accessible Seating Arrangements

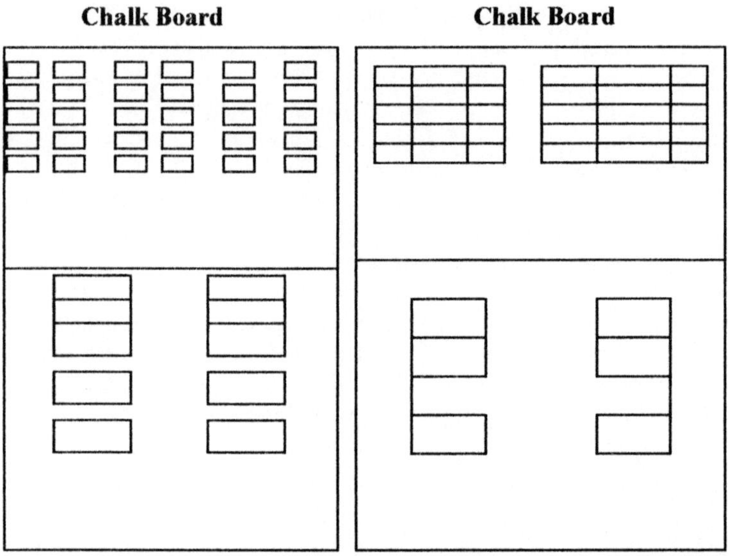

Chalk Board   **Chalk Board**

Part of establishing rapport in the classroom will necessitate that teachers become familiar with characteristic, traits and basic information relevant to student under his/her supervision. The following information may be collected through demographical information, hobbies and interests, data from observation and interviews. These data sources should be organized and recorded in some systematic way for future use.

Establishing rapport and trust require that both the teacher and children understand each other. As indicated, the teacher has at his/her disposal information to assist in understanding children. Children also need information to understand teachers. This joint understanding assists in forming a bond. When bonds are formed between teacher and children, discipline problems dissipate. Informing this bond, teachers need to discuss with students their interests, likes and dislikes. This open communication help students to see that teachers are not perfect and have some of the same needs and desires as children do. This will be an excellent time for the teacher to discuss his/her feelings and attitudes toward a variety of problems that he/she believes contributes to a positive classroom environment.

toward a variety of problems that he/she believes contributes to a positive classroom environment.

Classroom Control

A democratic teacher is one who can allow children freedom, but know when to set limits to their behaviors. When bonds are entrenched there is less need of the teacher to invoke limits. Edwards (1997) wrote that power, or control, is almost always an issue in the classroom. Students will assume all the power they can if realistic limits for their behaviors are not set. The effective teacher knows that children learn to accept responsibility, direction, and the need for structure and limits more readily when they are part of the decision making process. Effective teachers know to set limits and develop structure through the use of interpersonal powers that is democratic, confident and self-motivating to children. Children need some control and direction to assist them in becoming self-directed; the amount will vary depending upon the situation and the maturity level of the children. It should be the role of the teacher to assist children to become self-assured in hanging their behaviors (Jones, 1987a; 2000) contents that in addition to setting limits, giving clear instructions in the classroom are major factors in maintaining and managing classroom control.

Instructional Strategies

We have fully addressed this issue in Chapter 11. At this point only a summary of instructional strategies as related to discipline the classroom will be overviewed. Kauffman, Mostert, Trent & Hallahan (1998) contended that the simplest, most direct approach a teacher can take in using instruction, is telling the student what is expected. Te authors listed the following questions that teachers should ask themselves relevant to reducing discipline problems associated with the instructional program.

1. Have I made the instruction as simple and clear as possible?
2. Have I given the instruction in a clear, firm, non-tentative, but polite and non-angry way?
3. Have I made certain I have the student's full attention before giving instructions?
4. Have I given one instruction at a time?
5. Have I been careful not to give too many different instructions?
6. Have I waited a reasonable time for compliance before assuming that the instruction will not be followed?
7. Have I monitored compliance?

8.   Have I provided appropriate consequences for compliance?

Teachers will have to use their creativeness, combined with the needs and characteristic as well as experiment with various ways that they answer the questions. The instructions may have to be modified, modeled and practiced step by step with the children (Taylor, 1998). Refer to Chapters 3 – 9 for models to employ in modifying instructions.

Setting Limits

Teachers should combine instructional strategies with setting realistic and functional limits to assist children in improving their discipline. Effective limit techniques enable the teacher to correct inappropriate behaviors without verbal command and not embarrassing children. Some of the recommended strategies according to Edwards (1997) include:

1.   Monitoring the behavior of students. Teachers need to be able to predict behavior by using behavioral patterns for children. Children associate this type of behavior with the teacher having eyes in the back of his/her head;

2.   Terminating instruction. Jones view disruptions should be made during the instructional process to deal with inappropriate behavior, the discipline problem is reinforced. The teacher should in mid-sentence make a gesture to the student being assisted, stop the instruction and deal with the child making the inappropriate behavior (Jones, 1987b);

3.   Turning to face students signal to them that you are dealing with them solely. If teachers do not face students directly, students may conclude that the teacher is not serious about correcting the behavior. The students name should be said in a firm, calm voice, with the teacher directly facing the student, until the student reframes from engaging in the inappropriate behavior;

4.   Moving to the edge of the student's desk. When inappropriate behavior is noted, the teacher should move toward the student's desk in calm and relaxed manner. Stand at the desk and look the student straight in the eye and wait until the student returns to work;

5.   Moving out when the student's inappropriate behavior has stopped, and the student has returned to work, thank the student by name. Watch the student working for a while and move away slowly. The disruptive student will probably look up as if he is still being monitored. Teacher's

body language is a powerful medium for communicating expectations to students (Jones, 1993); and

6.   Using palms. If the student does not respond when a teacher stand in front of him/her, Jones recommends that the teacher should lean over at waist, and while resting your weight on one palm, give a short verbal or nonverbal prompt. If this does not work Jones recommends that the teacher use both palms with elbows locked, while maintaining continuous eye contact. Wait for a positive response or until the student returns to work.

Jones (1987a) indicated that sometimes during the setting limits sequence, students will engage in various types of back talk designed to get control and to trap the teacher to react. The author identified seven types of back talk.

a.   Feigning Helplessness. Students attempt to change the issue from discipline to instruction by pretending that they do not understand, and asks the teacher to demonstrate how to complete an assignment. Jones recommends that the teacher not provide assistance at the time, but say I will be back shortly to assist you. The less a teacher says concerning the request for assistance, the better.

b.   Denying Responsibility. Students sometimes deny responsibility for misbehaving when caught. Jones recommends that the teacher not respond to student's remarks, because responding only stimulates conflict. The teacher should simply do nothing. Just wait and relax.

c.   Blaming Others. Children use this strategy to shift the blame to another child. The strategy sometimes side track the teacher. The teacher tries to ascertain who is to blame so that corrective action can be taken. Jones reminded us that it does not matter who started the infractions. Students use this approach to avoid doing their work.

d.   Accusing the Teacher of Professional Incompetence. Students frequently use negative comments about teachers such you didn't explain well enough, or you did not make the assignment clear. The student's motive, according to Jones (1987a) is to side track the teacher. The student is attempting to avoid his/her responsibility not the quality of the instruction.

e. Urging the Teacher to Leave. When students make remarks to teachers such as "Ok just leave me alone", "Go away, I will do my work", "I am going to do this", they are attempting to control a situation and to get the teacher to react. Jones recommends that teacher ignore or not react to these behaviors.

f. Hurling Insults. Students may insult teachers when they feel that they have little to lose by insulting them. Teachers should relax and avoid over reacting to insults in order to control the situation.

g. Using Profanity. Students use profanity to provoke a reaction from teacher (Shearer, 1988). It is recommended when profanity is used in the classroom that the teacher set clears limits prohibiting the use of profanity and make sure that students understand the consequences of such an act. Teachers should remain clear and calm and not over react.

h. Camping Out in Front. This approach is not suited for all students, if step 6 has been effective. The teacher may band his/her arms and rest his/her weight on the elbows. This position will put the teacher in direct eye contact with the student. This position will usually cause the student to return to work.

i. Camping Out from Behind. This step may be used if students need to be separated. This step involves the teacher moving between students, turn sideways next to one student, and complete steps outlined in step 7.

The purpose of setting limits is to force students' compliance by teachers placing themselves in close proximity to students and forcing them into compliance. The technique assumes that the closer the teacher gets, the more intimidating the student will become and stop misbehaving. A word of caution is in order when using technique, some students may challenge the teacher and react violently to intrusion of their space.

Responsibility Training

Responsibility training is an alternative to punishment. This training is designed to promote students to show good behavior because they chose that most students will cooperate with the teacher if positive relationships are established and some reward is provided. The training is based on the concept of negative reinforcement, where students are given their rewards in advance. Jones calls his reward system Preferred Activity Time (PAT). PAT is given to the class as a whole in predetermined units, which the students can retain by demonstrating appropriate behaviors or loss through misbehavior. When a student misbehaves, the misbehavior is timed on a stopwatch by the teacher. The amount of time the misbehavior last is subtracted from the class PAT. Students may earn bonuses fro completing tasks before the allotted time. The teacher maintains a record of penalties and bonuses, and must make sure that the bonuses are more than bonuses the system will fail. The system has been successfully used controlling deviant behavior, in specialized classes, and outside the regular classroom. The effectiveness of the system depends upon student knowing the rules, and the teacher using a stopwatch to add bonuses on the subtract penalties.

Omission Training

Omission training may be used when PAT is not effective. It may be used with many individuals with disabilities, such as with emotional disabilities that show hostile and aggressive behaviors toward teachers and other students. Unlike responsibility training, omission training is based upon positive reinforcement. If the student behaves in a positive manner, a reward is given that can be shared with the total class. Four steps are employed in the training.

1.   Prevent any further confrontation by moving the student away from the rest of the class.
2.   Determine a period of time – from 15 minutes to an entire day – that you believe is reasonable and appropriate for the student to behave.
3.   Identify and communicate to the student the particular behavior you expect.
4.   Explain the bonuses that can be earned.

Back Up Systems

If neither responsibility on omission training is successful, the teacher should have a back up system which might consist of several strategies employed in a behavior modification system. (Refer to Chapter 6 for specific strategies to employ). Jones (1987a) recommends that teachers manage their own back-up system, independent of parents and

administrators because their participation is frequently unreliable and
assumes more time with minimal results.

Summary

Strengths of the Jones Model

1. It delineates a set of steps to follow in dealing with behavioral problems.
2. It sets the limits how far to go in applying behavioral techniques.
3. It defines the rules of all school personnel in using disciplinary measures.
4. The teacher has control of seating arrangements in the classroom.

Weaknesses of the Jones Model

1. It does not promote autonomy in students.
2. It is difficult for some teachers to apply the model as developed.
3. Some teachers are uncomfortable getting to close too students. Close physical proximity may also produce violent reactions in some children, causing some parents to intervene on behalf of their children (Kauffman, Mostert, Trent, & Hallahan, 1998).
4. The question of discipline taking preface over instruction needs further research to validate.
5. Punishing the total class for the misbehavior of a few students appears unjust.

Chapter 11

Improving Classroom Discipline

George R. Taylor

Overview

The effects of classroom management techniques are depleted throughout the processional literature. Generally, it is reported that classroom management has the greatest effect of student achievement, even more than cognitive processes, home environment and parental involvement, community impact, the culture, and instructional strategies (Wang, Haertel, & Walberg, 1994; Taylor, 1998).

These research findings indicated that specific strategies and structures must be developed to manage classroom behaviors. All classrooms are not created equally, that is special class room strategies are needed for children from diverse backgrounds, those from impoverish backgrounds, those in inclusive classroom, and parental management styles (refer to chapter 1 for specific details). Discipline is needed for all children. This is especially true for children from deprived backgrounds and special education specific strategies for improving the aforementioned strategies will be discussed with implications for all children.

There are many effective strategies that teachers can choose in reducing inappropriate behaviors in the classroom as articulated in chapters 3 – 9. According to Resnick, Bearman, Blum, Bauman, Harris, Jones, Tabor, Beuhring, Sieving, Shew, Ireland, Bearinger and Udry (1977). The two most important factors to reduce inappropriate behaviors in the classroom are positive emotional attachments to parents and teachers. The authors articulated that these relationships were more important then the size of classrooms, the type and amount of training teachers receive, classroom structures and rules, and administrative policy.

When students are treated fairly and feel as if they have some input in developing rules and determining consequences, they are most likely to conform to classroom rules and standards (Taylor, 2001).

Developing Positive Relationships

Developing positive relationship and connecting with students is one of the major steps that teachers and school personnel must employ in classroom management techniques. Derio (1996) research indicated how teachers can form positive relationship and connection with students through implementing the following strategies.

1. Creating one-to-one time with students through such activities as welcoming them back to school, greeting them on the first day of school with a hand shake and positive remarks, learning names soon and calling students by their names, develop strategies for having children learn each other names as quickly as possible, identify as quickly as possible the learning styles of children to assist them in learning.

2. Using self-disclosure to improve teacher-pupil relationships through revealing and sharing the teachers' own feelings, attitudes and experiences which will assist students in understanding the teachers views and perceptions toward issues and teaching strategies. Feedback from students concerning self-disclosure of the teacher is encouraged. The interactive style may be used to improve teaching and developing an atmosphere of trust in the classroom.

3. Having high expectations with a belief in students' abilities is a prime factor in promoting a positive classroom environment. Teachers and school personnel should set high standards and expectations for students. Teachers can ensure that students can achieve the standards and high positive expectations through modeling appropriate behaviors, permitting student lead conferences, and parental involvement all combine to assist students in reaching the expectations. Most children perform as teachers expect them to, both negative and positive behaviors.

4. Networking with family and friends appears to reduce factors which may give rise to inappropriate behaviors. When an avenue is created for involving parents, family, and peers, the student feels he/she is connected. This connectedness, according to Steinberg (1996) are important protective factors in reducing maladaptive behaviors.

5. Informed teachers find innovative ways of involving parents in the behavioral management of children by sending letters home, developing weekly newsletters, and involving parents in classroom activities (refer to Chapter 12 for strategies involving parents).

6. Building a sense of community in the classroom requires time and planning on the part of the teacher. A sense of community in the classroom must be built around the teacher connecting all students in his/her classroom. A first step would be to consider the unique characteristics of each child as to use this information to have a meaningful dialogue. Meaningful dialogues might immanent from individual conferences with students. Getting to know each student through dialoguing can build a strong teacher-student connection. This connection will assist students in internalizing their feeling and controlling inappropriate behaviors through self-management, which in essence will assist in creating a productive learning environment.

Creating An Effective Learning Environment

Arends (2000) wrote that the key to effective classroom management is having an effective learning environment which promotes and permits student engagement and participation. Creating an effective learning environment is no easy task. Teachers must be aware of the needs, interests and abilities of the class, and use this information to control behavior in the classroom. Arends (2000)* has provided excellent examples explaining the theoretical bases under pinning an effective learning environment. The reader is referred to the above source for specific information.

Classroom Structures

Several researchers, Kounin (1970), Doyle and Carter (1984), Johnson and Johnson (1994) and Slavin (1995), have all articulated that there is a direct correlation between the types of classroom structure imposed by teachers and behavior in the classroom. Teachers may change structures as his/her academic programs mandate. The various structures outlined by the aforementioned authors include: 1) task structures , 2) goals and reward structures, and 3) participation structures.

---

* Richard Arends. (2000). Learning to Teach. (5th Ed.) Boston: McGraw Hill.

Task Structures

These structures involve planned activities by teachers for students to perform cognitive and social tasks reflected in the curriculum. The nature and type of task depends upon the curriculum area under study, as well as the learning activities required by the teacher for students to complete. Arends (2000) example provides some clarity to the above, he stated that "sometimes different tasks demands exist within particular academic subjects. A lesson aimed at teaching multiplication tables in arithmetic for instance, makes a different set of demands in learners than does a lesson aimed at increasing skills in mathematical problem solving." Lack of the teacher modifying the task structures may cause students to become frustrated which in turn may lead to behavioral problems.

Goals and Reward Structures

According to Johnson and Johnson (1994) and Slavin (1995), goal structures refer the type of interdependence required of students as they attempt to complete learning tasks, as well as the relationship among students and between an individual and the group. The authors outlines three types of goal structures.

- Cooperative goal structures imply that students need the assistance of others to reach or achieve their goals. Cooperative learning strategies may be used to achieve goals.
- Competitive goal structures students are competing to achieve a state goal before others.
- Individualistic goal structures imply that achievement of goals is on an individual level. Achievement on goals is unrelated to group goals.

Under these structures students are rewarded for successfully achieving their goals. These structures have a significant impact on classroom behavior and learning in the classroom. Doyle (1979) contended that the way teachers organize goals and reward structures influence which types of goals are accomplished by students. Students whose goals and objectives are successfully met seldom create behavior problems.

Classroom Participation Structures

The importance of classroom participation in teaching and learning is well documented in the professional literature. Cazden (1986) articulated that participation structures denotes who can say what, when, and to whom, and include the way students take turns answering teachers questions and responding in-group discussions. It was further voiced by Cazden that these structures also vary from one type of lesson to another.

Several types of strategies may be employed to promote classroom participation, such as cooperative learning activities, and classroom discussion activities. When students are assisted in constructing their own learning activities and respond to standards and behaviors developed through group input, behavior problems are significant reduced.

Behavior Styles of Teachers

Several research studies have shown the effects of leadership in styles of teachers or behavior. Eleven-year old boys where exposed to three different forms of leadership style, authoritarian, laissez-faire, and democratic. Results showed that boys who participated in the authoritarian leadership demonstrated poorer interpersonal skills, such as being rebellious. Boys in the laissez-faire group, in the absence of structure stopped performing tasks. Boys in the democratic group continued to complete assigned tasks and provided leadership to the group. This study suggested that authoritarian and laissez-faire leadership styles by teachers may promote negative behaviors, where as, democratic leadership style promotes positive behavior (Arends, 2000; Lippitt and White, 1958).

Motivational Strategies to Improve Behavior

Students motivated to learn provide fewer behavior problems than those not motivated. Teachers must, therefore experiment with various forms of motivational strategies depending upon the unique needs of his/her classroom to assist students in controlling their behaviors. The following strategies to improve motivation have been advanced by Arends, 2000:

1.   *Believe in Students' Capabilities and Attend to Alterable Factors.* Teaching can significantly improve student motivation by accenting efforts on things that are within their abilities to control and influence, such as personalities, cultural and social values. Each child should be seen as a unique individual with the ability to learn regardless of his/her background. The teacher recognition of the values of diversity will do much to reduce negative behaviors in the classroom.

2.   *Avoid Over Emphasizing Extrinsic Motivation.* Rewarding children for positive behaviors can motivate them to produce desired behaviors needed to receive the reward. (We have reserved chapter 6 to expand this concept). Teachers should use caution when using extrinsic rewards because of the following consequences: 1) may reduce intrinsic motivations of students, 2) children may simply

display positive behaviors to receive the reward, 3) no intrinsic transfer of the value of the extrinsic behavior may occur, 4) children may not need extrinsic motivation to promote learning, which in term may promote behavior problems in the classroom.

3.   *Create Learning Situations with Positive Feeling Tones.* Research findings have clearly shown that classrooms that have positive feeling tones, and tasks completed by children are viewed as pleasant rather than unpleasant by the teacher tend to motivate students to complete assign task in a timely manner. Teachers should practice using positive tones when remarking about school related issues. Negative feelings tones may contribute to behavior problems (Santrock, 1976; Marshall,   1987; Arends, 2000).

4.   *Build on Students' Interests and Intrinsic Values.* Teachers should assess children to determine values and information they bring in the learning environment.   Determining interests of children and using the information in the instructional program can significantly improve children's intrinsic values, and facilitate learning in the classroom (Taylor, 1999). Teacher may use a variety of strategies and resources to correlate learning tasks to children's interests, such as: 1) relating instruction to the experiences of the children, 2) relating experiences to the cultural values of the children, 3) use resources that are within the cultural experiences of the children, 4) use a variety of human and physical resources to augment the instructional program, such as field trips., and guest speakers. When the interest of children is considered in the instruction program, behavior problems are few.

5.   *Attend the Structure of Learning Goals and Difficulty of Instructional Task.* Learning goals and instructional tasks which are to difficult or to easy may attribute to negative behaviors in the classroom. When learning tasks (difficult or easy) do not motivate students all types of problems may surface. Teachers should be aware of the unique learning styles of children and adjust the level of difficulty of learning so that each child can achieve the stated objectives. This may necessitate developing difficult time lines for children to complete assigned tasks.

6.   *Establish Realistic Rules and Routine.* Rules and routines should be established with input from children. Consequences for not following the rules and routines should also have student input. Rules and routines should be constantly reviewed. It is incumbent upon teachers to make sure that rules, routines and consequences of behaviors are fully understood by children, regardless of the structure and type of classrooms in which children are placed.(Taylor, 2001).

Multi-Age Classrooms

In these classrooms, students stay with the same teacher for two or more grades. Proponents of this approach believe that under this structure children would receive more individualize attention and teachers will have more time for bonding (Veenman, 1995). Another aspect of a multi-age classroom is looping. In this structure, students are in a single grade class with the same teachers for two or more years. In both structures classroom management should be well established because children will be accustomed to the classroom structure and rules. One who suspects less behavior problem in these structures premised upon the above.

Practicing Self-Control

A proactive approach should be practice by teacher and school related personnel to teach anger management. It is practically impossible to teach anger management when students are emotionally involved in aggressive behaviors. During discussion groups, students can discuss ways of reducing anger, such as mediation, compromise, negotiation, ways to ignore teasing, and problem solving techniques. These techniques may be demonstrated through role playing, creative dramatic, view tapes and films, playing games, taking deep breaths, modeling by teachers, and internalizing the consequences of the behavior. Research findings by Johnson, Johnson, Dudley, Wand, Magnuson (1995) showed that students who participated in anger management techniques were able to problem solve and find solutions to conflicts without resorting to aggressive behaviors. Teachers must provide strategies to make children aware of their anger by assisting them in internalizing it. If one is not aware of anger, it cannot be controlled.

Controlling anger and managing feelings are essential in developing appropriate interpersonal skills. Children should be taught to control anger through application or the following strategies:

1.   Recognizing and describing negative responses and anger.

2. Finding appropriate ways to express anger or negative response.
3. Analyzing and understanding factors responsible for anger through critiquing some of the activities noted above.
4. Managing anger by looking at events differently in talking one self out of anger.
5. Learning how to express feeling in a positive way.
6. Experimenting with various ways of controlling anger.

A variety of strategies may be used by teachers and related school personnel to assist children in controlling or reducing anger. In addition to strategies already mentioned, time out, relaxation therapy, waiting and talking out feeling, assertive behavioral techniques, and cooperative approaches and strategies may be used by the teacher to reduce and control anger of children (Taylor, 1997).

Proactive Interventional Strategies

A proactive approach is recommended for teachers to use in managing discipline problems in the classroom and school (Kandel, 2000). Some guidelines and strategies that teachers can employ are similar to those advanced by Arends (2000) earlier in the chapter. When you ask a student in your class, on the playground, or in the hallways to do something, most will obey you. However, there are times when you ask a student to comply with school rules or make a request and the student confidently, and without hesitation, responds, "NO." This about the time when a minor altercation erupts into a major problem that could result in the student being reprimanded, given detention, or suspended. How can we deal with children who say "NO?" Better yet, what can we do to prevent the child from being in a situation where he/she has the opportunity to say "NO?" By implementing the following strategies and guidelines, teachers and educators can significantly reduce the situation for children to say "NO."

1. *Establish Classroom Rules.* Developing sound classroom rules, posting them, and reviewing them daily will go a long way to preventing potential problems. Try to write rules with your students, so they will begin to take ownership. Write the rules in a positive way. For example, rather than the rule, "No running," rewrite that statement in a positive way: "Please walk at all times." It's human nature to be turned off by a series of rules or regulations in which each statement begins with "NO."

    Also, make your rules specific. "Be prepared for class" does not communicate to your students your expectations.

Rather, the rule, "Come to class with your pencil, pen, books, and paper" leaves no doubt as to what you expect. One final note on rules and procedures. Keep your rules to a maximum of five, and make sure the are observable and measurable.

2. *Promote Smooth Transitions.* Often students will respond negatively to your commands when they feel pressured to move from one activity to another without sufficient forewarning. Some students will need more preparation than others. Get to them first and begin to move them along so you don't reach a point that becomes confrontational. Also, cue, or signal, students that an activity is coming to an end. And, use close proximity to encourage students to follow your commands rather than putting them on the spot in front of their peers.

3. *Know the Function of the Student's Behavior.* It is extremely important that you determine the underlying cause or goal of a student's behavior. We can be effective with an appropriate intervention only when we recognize the purpose the student's behavior serves. For example, if a student responds to your command with an "NO," is he/she looking for attention? You may respond by keeping the child in for lunch or recess. On the surface, your actions may appear to be a punishment for the student; however, the child enjoys what he/she perceives as some time alone with you.

Is the student trying to escape a situation or demand? You may escalate a situation to the point where you send the child to the office. Once again, you view this as a punishment. On the other hand, this seventh grade boy, who is a poor reader, just escaped the humiliating experience of reading orally in your class.

Finally, is the child responding in a negative way to gain power or control? You may win this confrontational "battle" because you moved the child to time-out, send him/her to the office, or assign detention. However, you have lost the "war," because every student now knows what buttons to push to get you into such a state.

First, you need to know your students and their "triggers," what words, actions, or phrases seem to put them into a heightened state of anxiety or defensiveness? For example, some children do not respond well to requests early in the morning. Others need to be presented a request in a manner that doesn't appear to be a request. Remember, communication is 80 percent "how" something is said and 20 percent "what" is said.

In addition to knowing the "trigger," you need to know the underlying function of a child's behavior. Is the child responding in a negative way to get attention, seek power and control, receive a tangible, or escape/avoid a situation or demand? More than likely children who respond to commands with a "NO" are trying to gain power to control. They may also be trying to gain a degree of independence. There are several strategies a teacher can use to deal with students who say "NO," keep in mind, these strategies should be used with other proactive intervention.

4. *Refrain from Escalating a Minor Incident.* Often we as teachers share responsibilities for escalating a minor incident into a major problem. To reduce the risk of escalating a situation with a student, try to deal in the present. Stay away from reminding the student of past failures and problems.

Talk directly to the student rather than about the student. Be sure to make eye contact, but don't force your student to "look at you when you are speaking," Unless they are hard of hearing, they can hear you. It is humiliating for any of us to look our accusers in the eye when we know are wrong.

Finally, make statements rather than ask questions. Teachers have a habit of asking the wrong question in a tense situation (How many times do I have to tell you to stop talking?) and getting an unexpected answer from a student ("Tell me 10 more times and I will stop").

5. *Give Choices Whenever Possible.* If the circumstance permits, allow your students to have a choice in their daily routines and activities. If a student believes they have some choice in a situation, they feel more independent and may be less likely to confront you with a "NO." For example, if you want students to complete a math and social studies assignment before recess, why not let them chose which assignment they will do first?

Assessing student knowledge also gives you an opportunity to give them a choice. For example, some students may opt for a written test, while others want to create a project. By incorporating students' interests into our daily routines, we give them opportunities to exert some independence and reduce their need to seek power and control by negative means.

6.   *Remove the Student.* This is easier said than done. Invent creative ways to remove the student from the current situation without you or the student "losing face." It may mean you will have to redirect him or her by sending the child on an errand. You need to plan for these situations. You will not be successful if you try to think on your feet when you have locked horns with a student in front of 28 peers.

7.   *Remove the Audience.* Sometimes it is not advisable to remove a student from your classroom. You may have to look for ways to remove the other students. This can be done within the room (e.g., direct your students' attention to a different part of the room: blackboard, overhead) or outside of the room (having students stand in the hallway). While the audience is removed, attempt to de-escalate the situation and come to a temporary solution.

With these last two strategies, it is imperative that you keep other options available, including involving the administration. You need to have planned in advance how to deal with a student who will not remove himself or herself from the room. Don't put yourself or your students in danger.

8.   *Agree with the Student.* The next time a student responds "NO" and tells you that "you can't make me do it," simply agree with him/her. It is very difficult to argue with someone when they agree with you. By remaining calm and businesslike, you have removed the bait and left the student fishing for another. Understand that the student will likely want to continue to argue. State to the student what you expect, no more. For example, I expect you to do problems one through 10 and turn them in at the end of class. Remove yourself and allow some space. If the child refuses to comply, restate, your demand with a consequence. "You can sit quietly and do problems one through 10, or you will lose recess. "Another consequences for students who

continue to act out may be to send them to time out or the office.

Be careful here. Again, it's important that you know the underlying function of the student's behavior. Is the child saying "NO" to gain power/control, or is he/she looking to be removed from the room (escape/avoid)? If he/she is trying to escape or avoid, that situation/demand may indicate the child is experiencing difficulty with the assignment.

9.   *Contact Parents ASAP.* It's very important to keep an open line of communication with your students' families. Equally important is to communicate on a consistent basis when your students are exhibiting appropriate behaviors. By doing this, you will be more likely to have parental cooperation when a student engages in inappropriate behavior.

Make parental contact on the first offense. Do not let the misbehavior go in second offense without discussing it with the student's parents.

Inevitably you will encounter students who, when you make a request or demand, will respond with "NO." Be proactive in anticipating these situations and what may trigger them for certain students. Become skilled at identifying the goal or function of a child's misbehavior and develop strategies to address his/her needs. Don't allow your actions to escalate a minor incident into a major problem.

As the teacher and authority figure in the classroom, know your limits of power. You can't make kids do or think anything they don't want to. Establish a positive classroom environment and provide your students with choices to help them (Jackson & Owens, 1999).

Summary

Teachers need practical strategies for improving discipline in the classroom. They need to be apprised of problems that may cause discipline problems and to use strategies to reduce them. It is recommended that teachers develop strategies suited to the individual needs and characteristics of children under his/her supervision. A recommended universal concept is "proactive." Be being proactive, many discipline problems will never surface. This chapter was designed to reflect how teachers and school officials can improve discipline in the classroom through employing proactive techniques and strategies.

Participation of students and parents in managing classroom behavior is deemed essential.

Chapter 12

Classroom Management and Instruction

Lois Nixon

Effective classroom management strategies are based upon teachers creating a democratic environment where student's participation is sough and valued. Classroom management is considered one of the most challenging task facing new teachers. Many new teachers fail because they are not able to employ effective classroom management techniques in dealing with student behaviors. Since classroom management techniques are highly correlated with instruction, a teacher lacking in classroom management techniques will likely have an ineffective instructional program. On the other hand, a teacher who has n effective instructional program, based upon the needs, interests and learning styles of the students, is likely to have good classroom organization and control (Taylor, 1998).

Children receive and order information differently and through a variety of dimensions and channels . Teachers must assess and determine the type of learning style a child uses the best, cognitive, affective, physiological and psychological, and develop instructional strategies to meet the need. (For additional information refer to Taylor, 1999). * Many behavior problems are caused when the learning styles of children do not match the instructional program (Taylor, 1998). Early identification, assessment, and management of learning styles, needs

---

*George R. Taylor. (1999). Curriculum Models and Strategies for Educating Individuals with Disabilities in Inclusive Classroom. Springfield, IL, Charles C. Thomas.

and interests of children can prevent serious behavior problems from occurring, providing that the teacher employs learning style information of students in his/her instructional process. By keying teaching and assessment techniques to ways children think and learn will improve the learning environment.

Organized Instructional Strategies

Instructional strategies must be organized to assist students in internalizing their behaviors. Strategies should be employed which promotes children to develop appropriate social skills needed to control their behaviors. Social skills are numerous and cover a wide variety of human and behavioral skills, such as 1) interpersonal skills, 2) positive self-concept skills, 3) identifying and evaluating the feelings of others, and 4) using appropriate communication skills are to name but a few. These skills can be easily infused into the existing curriculum.

Additionally, instructional strategies, in order to be effective in managing behaviors, must reflect the behavioral objectives articulated by the teacher or the school. Achievement of the objectives to manage behaviors may be realized through dramatic play, role-playing, modeling, and the use of audio-visual equipment. The real and functional activities will provide additional ways in which students may effectively and appropriately deal with behavioral problems in the classroom and the school.

Social competency is an important aspect of interrelationships. The experience of interacting with others is necessary for a well-managed classroom. Children need to be taught to acknowledge, notice, value, respect, and appreciate teachers, administrators, school staff and their peers (Taylor, 1999). Activities and creative games may be designed to improve social greetings, developing positive relationships, respecting the feelings and rights of others, practicing common courtesy, acceptable ways to show anger, practicing self-control and learning when an apology is needed. Activities of the school should be age appropriate and modified and adapted as the teacher sees fit (Edwards, 1997).

Motivational Strategies

Student must see a need and be motivated to behavior appropriately in the classroom, the school and the community. A supportive, organized classroom environment, meaningful age-appropriate materials and resources, and task-oriented, rather than ego-oriented classrooms are necessary preconditions that must be met in order to motivate children and have effective classroom management. See suggested strategies in Appendix E.

A supportive, organized classroom environment provides an ideal environment for teachers to use motivational strategies. A clearly organized classroom structure with consistent expectations helps students feel secure and decreases anxiety (Jones & Jones, 1989). Be as positive with students as possible, use statements that promote acceptance, and encourage and reward peers' for giving positive support to each other. Survey students' feelings about being in your classroom, and attend to their suggestions for making it a more comfortable, safe environment.

A second important precondition is to ensure that the difficulty level of the materials and the pace of instruction are appropriate. It is difficult to motivate students to learn when using materials that are too difficult or employed at an inappropriate instructional pace.

When students' skill levels differ, use a variety of materials so that all students feed challenged but able to succeed. In addition to difficulty level, ensure the materials are meaningful to students and that they reflect their backgrounds and interests (Edwards, 1999).

Competitive environments, in which success is defined by outperforming other students, are not conducive to motivational strategies. Since most students with disabilities do not perform at the top of the class, many will not feel that they can succeed. Instead, create a "task-oriented" classroom environment in which all students strive to improve over their previous performance and in which effort and attention are encouraged and rewarded rather than performing better than others.

Techniques for Improving Behavior

The many techniques for improving motivation include improving self-efficacy, increasing personal investment in learning, making learning enjoyable, and using praise and rewards (Campbell, J., 1999).

Increase Self-Efficacy

Self-efficacy is described as confidence in one's abilities to succeed. Students are more motivated to participate when they have a high degree of self-efficacy (Taylor, 1998). Self-effficacy can be enhanced by structuring tasks that your students can complete with reasonable effort and a high rate of success. As your students increase their history of success, they will increase their desire to engage in new tasks. When you are presenting new tasks, remind your students of how successful they have been on similar tasks in the past.

State your confidence in your students' ability to succeed with statements such as, "I feel certain you can do this really well if you try hard." When your students succeed, remind them of your previous confidence in them. However, refrain from characterizing tasks as "easy," by saying, "You can do this, it's easy!" Little satisfaction can be obtained from succeeding at an "easy" task, and failing at an easy task can be humiliating. If a student who is successful characterizes the task as easy, you could say something like, "Well, maybe it was easy for you, because you knew the material so well, but I really don't think it was that easy."

Increase Personal Investment in Learning

Students are more motivated when their personal investment in learning is increased. One way of doing this is through goal setting. Show your students examples of their previous work, and ask them to set a goal for their future performance. Students can set daily, weekly, or monthly goals for themselves. For example, they can set goals for how many math problems they can complete correctly in one period, how many words they can spell correctly on a weekly test, or their score on a unit test in history. Provide positive feedback when your students meet their goals, and encourage them to set higher goals, and encourage them to set higher goals for themselves in the future. Also, help your students monitor their own progress toward longer-term goals (Zlatos, 1994).

Attribution training is another way to help students increase their investment in their learning. Teach your students' to attribute their successes to things they are in control of, such as effort, planning, or use of appropriate learning strategies. Enforce this thinking with statements such as, "The reason you did so well on that test is that you planned your time carefully and studied really hard!" Conversely, when students do not succeed, do not accept negative attributions such as "I'm stupid" or "It's too hard." Redirect learning failures to things under the students' control, and encourage better efforts in the future.

Finally, you can increase your students' investment in the classroom by increasing student decision-making in classroom procedures. Solicit your students' suggestions for class rules, seating arrangements, or learning activities, and implement these suggestions whenever possible. Remind your student that many classroom procedures are influenced by their own suggestions.

Make Learning Fun

Students are more motivated to learn when classroom tasks are fun and enjoyable. Few things are less motivating than a seemingly endless stack of worksheets. Use materials that are concrete, meaningful, and relevant to your students; lives. Develop activities that are fun for students, and allow them to actively participate in the concepts being learned (Taylor, 1999). When drill is necessary, as in some basic skills areas, provide fast-paced, high-energy activities in which success rates are high, students are rewarded for learning, and activities are conducted within discrete time intervals.

Other ways to make learning fun and enjoyable include providing variety in class activities, through, for example, different media, guest speakers, student presentations, and computer applications. Create variety in homework assignments, and employ a variety of group and individual activities.

Develop classroom activities in game like formats. Competition that pits student against student can be counterproductive to a classroom environment, but activities in which any student has a good chance of winning can be very motivating. Activities in which groups compete (on, e.g., questions about the current science chapter), and in which group membership changes frequently, can be particularly enjoyable for your students (Cummings, 2000)

Finally, make learning enjoyable by teaching enthusiastically. You can do this by increasing inflections in your speaking, using dramatic body movements and physical gestures, employing animated and motive facial expressions, using a varied choice of words, and actively accepting student ideas or suggestions. Overall, a demonstration of a high energy level promotes enthusiasm. When teachers teach with enthusiasm, students are more motivated to learn.

Use Praise and Rewards

We saved praise and rewards until last because it is usually the first thing teacher's thing about when trying to increase motivation. Nevertheless, it is very true that students are more motivated to learn when they think they will be rewarded for their efforts. Be generous with praise and positive feedback; most of use receive too little praise rather than too much. Be sure to link praise to specific criteria students have met, and link it to positive attributions such as effective study strategies and extra effort. Instill in your students a sense of personal satisfaction with statements such as, "This is your best effort yet! You should be very proud of this paper!" Inform parents of particularly noteworthy student efforts.

More tangible rewards also can promote motivation in your students. When using more tangible rewards, such as redeemable tokens, stickers, or special privileges, be sure to set up conditions for the rewards, include specific performance criteria, and pair rewards with positive attributions. Be careful not to provide tangible rewards more than necessary, and be sure external rewards do not take the place of the personal satisfaction students should feel in doing a job well. As withal motivational strategies, collect evidence that your efforts are yielding positive results (Taylor, 2001).

Motivation may be the most important single characteristic to promote in students to help ensure their long-term success. Motivated students are generally successful students, and it is worth our own best efforts to bring out the best efforts of our students. Motivation strategies are outline in Appendix E.

Preventive Classroom Management Problems

There are several preventive strategies that teachers can employ to prevent classroom management problems. A proactive rather than a reactive approach is needed. The following proactive strategies are recommended:

1. Establish with children commonly agreed rules and classroom procedures. Rules and procedures should be modeled by teachers and taught to children. Additionally, consequences of not following rules should also be taught to children. (Refer to Appendix F).

2. Maintain consistency in reinforcing rules and procedures. Avoiding a difficult situation may lead to a complex problem later. Equal reinforcement should be applied for all infractions of the rules or procedures, based upon the premise that children have been involved and initially agreed to the consequences. Teacher must maintain consistency in applying rules and procedures in the classroom, if not children will become confused in following rules and procedures in the classroom.

    Teachers must become skilled observers and develop systematic strategies for recording behavior. This information may assist the teacher in pinpointing the conditions and time certain types of behaviors are more likely to occur and plan intervention strategies for reducing or correcting the behavior, such as using rewards and praises.

3. Pacing the instructional program. Keep the flow of activities at a level of momentum with the needs, abilities and interests of the children. The teacher must consider and be aware of his/her own behavior in interfering with the flow of activities, such as not giving complete direction for completing an activity, not allowing enough time to complete an activity, changing directions for completing an activity. Pacing becomes very important when all students

need to learn the same material at the same time. The teacher must realize that some students will be able to master the materials faster. In this case the more advanced students can assist their peers. The teacher must determine an appropriate pace for his/her class. It is a pace which meets the requirement of appropriately 75% of the class is adequate. However, this pace will be slow for the most advanced learner, but it will keep the lesson moving along and provide success for most of the students. Students who are unable to keep up will require assistance from the teacher or peers.

4.   Develop strategies for preventing deviant behaviors. Several strategies are recommended for preventing deviant behaviors. The teacher should choose these strategies based on the nature and type of behavior being demonstrated. There should be no particular order for employing these strategies.

- Greeting children at the door assist in building positive reactions and may reduce potential problems.
- Assigning and providing assigned tasks for student to complete in the classroom, rotate student helpers frequently.
- Developing cuing signs to manage behaviors such as hand signals, finger signals, bell signals, light signals, folding arm signals and voice signals have all been used to prevent behavior problems once students have been augmented to them.

5.   Explain tasks and assignments clearly to students. In some instances demonstrating and modeling may be needed. Teachers should be prompt in checking assignments as well as providing timely feedback to students. A well-organized and structured classroom leaves little room for behavior problems to occur.

Off Task Behaviors

Examples of off task behaviors include students talking to one another during times allocated for listening to a presentation, interrupting a speaker, being discourteous, clowning, and acting violently are usually considered to be disruptive behaviors. Other types of off-task behaviors may be considered as nondisruptive, examples include daydreaming, being inattentive, failing to complete homework, skipping class, and cheating on examinations. When behaviors interfere with on-task behaviors of other students they made be labeled as disruptive. Charles & Senter (1995) alluded that disruptive behaviors are the source of most teachers greatest fears when disruptive behaviors occurs frequently, teachers are considered to have poor classroom control. By employing activities in "The Teaching Process Model" many disruptive behaviors can be systematically controlled.

On Task Behaviors

Teachers must be aware of individual differences in motivating students to be on-task strategies must suit the individual style of each student. Activites should be individualized, and designed to promote: 1) interest in learning, 2) self-confidence, 3) perception of what is important, 4) positive attitude toward school, 5) positive aptitude for reasoning, 6) prior achievement, 7) experiences upon which teachers can build on based upon the different background of students, 8) home and school life, 9) cultural understanding, 10) effects of substance abuse, 11) accommodating exceptionalities, 12) working with non-English proficient students, 13) strategies and activities to reduce antisocial behaviors, 14) recognizing different learning styles, 15) matching learning styles with instructional styles, 16) modeling behaviors, and 17) giving students adequate response time (Cummings, 1984; Doyle, 1979). Developing appropriate on-task behaviors for students is involved and time consuming for teachers. They will need detailed and specific information relevant to each child. The teacher's process model is a recommended strategy to use in promoting on task behaviors.

Research findings by Kounin (1970) revealed that it is easier to prevent discipline problems than to deal with them once they occur. A proactive rather than a reactive approach is recommended. Teachers using a proactive approach were better able to keep children on task. They employ the following strategies:

1. Started instructions with highly motivated activities,
2. Asked students probing questions to stimulate their thinking and interest.
3. Have students to respond to their classmate's responses to questions.
4. Planned functional and interesting seatwork by making sure that students understand how to complete the seatwork and have the necessary materials and resources available.
5. Give immediate and specific feedback to student concerning their performances so that will know how to correct mistakes on move on to a higher level.

6.   Handle class disruptions quickly and effectively (Kounin, 1970) indicated that teachers must know how to target most disruptive behaviors and use proper timing in correcting them. They must know at all times what is going on in the classroom. If teachers ruin the risk of not being able to maintain classroom control. See Appendix H.

The Physical Environment

Like the psychological environment, the physical environment can contribute to behavior problems in the classroom. The physical arrangement of the classroom must be arranged to maximize learning, through group and individual activities (Jones, 1987a) supported this view. They found that when students' desks were in the front and center of the classroom (action zone) they performed better than their classmates seated in other areas, stayed on task longer, and had better attitudes. The implication of this research is that teachers should periodically change the seating arrangement to the action zone.

Different seating arrangements influence behavior indifferent ways. Desk arrangements provide the opportunity for shaping student-teacher interactions articulated that students maintained greater on-task behavior and participated more actively when their seat desks were arranged in a circular pattern, on the other hand students seated in rows were more likely to participate less in discussions and engage in less on-tasks behaviors.

Classrooms should be safe, secure, warm and comfortable places for children to learn. It is incumbent upon the teacher to create the aforementioned conditions. Studies have shown that the quality of the classroom environment reflects the personality trait of the teacher. When the teachers' personality becomes autocratic, students become involved in more conflicts with peers. Student in insecure classrooms are prone to show more feelings of fatigue and discontent (Jones, 1987b).

Effective Schools

According to most research effective schools have:

1.   A positive et hos where students are taught both intellectual and moral development (Taylor, 1999).
2.   A classroom climate conducive to learning when parents, teachers, administrators and students create a positive climate for learning (Kines, 1999).
3.   Have clearly understood goals and objectives which have to be developed and understood by teachers, parents, administrators and students(Cangelos, 1997).

4. Effective teaching where teachers are well organized, routinely assign and grade homework, have friendly but authoritative relation with students, make effective use of class time (Cangelos, 1997).

5. Clear and effective leadership. Good administrators ensure that teachers can carry out their instructional programs without serious interruptions, supply the necessary materials and resources to carry out the instructional program, and provide opportunities for faculty development (Anderson & Decker, 1993).

6. Good communication. There is a constant flow of information between all stakeholders. Parents are equal partners in planning and executing the instructional program. Parents are also involved in the supervision of students' homework (Davies, 1996).

7. Students should be actively involved in the operation of the school and function in leadership roles in directing activities such as awards assemblies, pep rallies and other school related activities (Davies, 1996).

8. Incentives and rewards for honoring students and faculty who have demonstrated a high level of achievement.

9. Good order and discipline. These school enforce dress codes with the approval of all stakeholders. They also have traditions that they respect and use and involve all stakeholders in social affairs conducted at the school.

Summary

The values of effective classroom management in reducing discipline problems has been projected throughout this chapter. A proactive rather than reactive approach was recommended and several successful strategies were outlined for teachers to follow in managing the classroom.

The importance of the physical environment in the learning process was summarized. The role of the instructional program in managing classroom behavior indicate the importance of effective instructional strategies in reducing inappropriate behaviors.

Classroom management strategies are essential to the instructional program. The success or failure of new teachers can be attributed to his/her classroom management skills. These classroom management skills may be based upon a behaviorist, cognitive, or child center approach. Regardless of the approach used, children should be involved as much as possible in the standards, rules and consequences imposed. Teacher must also examine their own behaviors to determine if they are attributing to the behavior problems through their attitudes, structure and strict behavior patterns.

Research findings discussing characteristic of effective schools showed that strategies developed and implemented by stakeholders can promote effective classroom management. In effective schools, strong and effective administration is essential. An administration can make or break a school's positive climate.

Chapter 13

Parenting Skills: Impact Upon Behavioral Patterns of Children

George R. Taylor

The importance of parenting cannot be overlooked by the schools. Parents are the child's first teachers. The parental role in the family therefore focuses on being a role model for the child. In the early formative stage of a child, the actions of parents or adults are modeled by children. It is at this point in a child's life that the quality of parental behavior is critical. Parents, who express warmth, happiness, consideration, and respect in their daily handling of the child are acknowledged to be assisting the child in developing a positive approach to problems. Parents should provide model behaviors that they wish their children to demonstrate (Dunst, Trivett, Hamby, & Pollock, 1990). If parents do not provide guidance by personal example of their major values, it is difficult to help a child emulate desired behaviors (Cullingford, 1996).

In essence, behaviors parents wish their children to exhibit in their adult lives should be a reflection of their own behaviors. The primary parental role in the family is that of being a teacher of trust. Quite often, society has witnessed many children who have no confidence in their families or themselves; hence the choose alternate support groups as a family. Parents need to have confidence that giving emotional support to their children will enable them to cope with the demands of family, friends, school, and society.

Dealing with the confidential aspect of the child's life is one of the most essential arts of parenting. At this time, children are taught to have confidence and reliance on themselves. Parents are advised to intervene in whatever practicable way to influence their children's behavior; to set limits, shape behaviors, and engage in mental problem solving discussions (White & White, 1992). Parenting, therefore, requires parents to provide skills which will equip their children to function appropriately in society.

Parenting is not about beautiful things all the time. It is about good and bad, the fulfilling and draining, the rewarding and the punishing. With respect to this, parenting practically depends on how well parent grow with their children and help their children to become positive individuals. To build this confidence, parents need to exhibit self-confidence in the presence of their children.

Respect is a major art of parenting. Parenting is a most stimulating job that requires wisdom, sensitivity, strength, and endurance. To be effective, parents must respect their children as human beings. In some cases, children turn to undesirable elements because their parents do not set appropriate models for them to emulate. The mind set of children is conditioned primarily by how their parents respect or regard them (Caldwell, 1997).

Children need to be interacted with and talked to with as much respect, courtesy, and consideration as you would expect for oneself. Yelling at children has a deteriorating effect on them. To receive respect and cooperation from children, parents should respect their individual rights.

Love and discipline are among other arts of parenting. Although, it is advisable for parents to love their children, it must be expressed in ways that are beneficial for their children and comfortable for the parents. Discipline is a form of love, and parents should learn how to use it to avoid letting love for the child cloud the responsibility of parenting. Discipline guidelines for parents are listed in Appendix G.

Communication is a form of parenting. Parents who communicate well with their children create, in a practical form, a direct channel for closeness and development of a positive self-concept which will be needed for later school success (Taylor, 2000). Children who experience all or part of the aforementioned develop confidence about themselves that carries over to many other situations or difficulties that they may face. A woman who experienced good communication and a warm relationship with her own parents always look forward with confidence to her own mothering, and there is every likelihood that she will pass her good experience on to her children.

The importance of parenting in this family relies on commitments, providing warmth and nurturing for all members, and encouraging the development of difficulties. The challenge in parenting is to relate to children with disabilities, as well as to children without disabilities, in manners and ways that stimulate their potentialities for growth and provide appropriate opportunities for experiences that develop these potentialities. Parenting skills in various cultures differ. Educators and teachers should be aware of the various culture styles and adjust instructional programs and school activities to reflect diversity (Okagaki & French, 1998; Taylor, 1997).

Parental involvement in the school can also be expedited through scheduling periodical conferences. This will provide opportunities for the teachers to assess the parents' skills and completeness for working in the classroom. As parents become familiar with the behavioral programs at school, they may reinforce the skills taught to their children at home. Under supervision, the parents may develop or establish a behavior management program at home to augment the school's program.

Armstrong (1991) informed us that parental involvement is essential in assisting the school in developing appropriate social and educational skills for children. He concluded that involving parents in academic social skills homework transferring of skills functional and realistic for children.

Parental Involvement in the Classroom

Parents who conduct tasks in the classroom should receive some type of advanced preparation and orientation. During this orientation, parents should be provided with the school's mission, philosophy, and behavioral program. Additionally, they should be apprised of: 1) the class schedules, 2) the school calendar, 3) official meetings, 4) resources and supplies, 5) extracurricular activities, 6) in-service training and provisions for working parents, 7) conference schedules, 8) food and snacks, 9) evaluation and progress reports, and 10) advanced notices of services needed. Many parents can serve as valuable resources in the classroom.

Classroom Behavior

The classroom provides a structure for the child to demonstrate both appropriate and inappropriate behavior (Taylor, 1999). Teachers need to make known to parents, methods and procedures, which will be employed to evaluate the child's behavior. This assessment requires professional judgment on the part of the teacher to accurately and objectively report the behavior. Detailed knowledge of development norms in the areas of intelligence, social/emotional and physical development are needed in order for the teacher to make a valid report on the child's classroom behaviors. Parents should have an opportunity to observe the child in the classroom. They should plan with the teacher strategies for improving or modifying the behavior. When communicating with parents relevant to classroom behaviors, the teacher can compare performance of the child with another child of the same age. However, some caution is in order. Children of the same age may perform well above or below the normative group. The recommended approach would be to use the child as his or her own yardstick and assess his or her learning styles to progress over a certain time frame.

During reporting and conference time, the teacher should discuss with the parent the procedures used to evaluate the child, noting reasons why the child is performing above or below the expected age level of his or her peers and how the learning style was assessed. It is essential, during the conference, that the teacher accent the positive behaviors of the child and encourage the parents to reinforce those behaviors at home. For negative behaviors, strategies should be discussed to minimize or eradicate the behaviors. Before ending the discussion, reporting period, or conference, teachers and parents should agree on the following:

1. What can be done at school and home to improve the child's social/emotional development?
2. Timelines and location for the next conference with an area for discussion.
3. Parents should leave the conference with some idea on how the behavioral strategies will be achieved, as well as his/her role in the process in improving behavior and promoting social skills (Taylor, 2000).

Developing Pro-Social Skills/Behaviors

Research from social learning theory implies that pro-social learning theory implies that pro-social behaviors of children are enhanced when behavioral expectations are clearly specified and reinforced with praise, encouragement, and other positive acts by parents and teachers. (Refer to Table 13.1 for specific examples.)

Table 13.1

Ninety-two (92) Ways to Promote Academic and Social Growth of Children with Disabilities

I. You're doing a good job?
2. You did a lot of work today!
3.Now you've figure it out.
4.That's RIGHT!!!
5.Now you've got the hang of it!
6. That's the way!
7. You're doing fine!
8. Now you have it!
9. Nice going.
10. You're really going to town.
11. That's great
12. You did it that time.
13. GREAT!
14. FANTASTIC!
15. TERRIFIC!
16. Good for you.
17. GOOD WORK!
18. That's better.
19. EXCELLENT!
20. Good job, (name of student)
21. You outdid yourself today.
22. That's the best you've done ever.
23. Good going.
24. That's really nice.
25. Keep it up!
26. WOW!!
27. Keep up the good work.
28. Much better.
29. Good for you.
30. That's much better.
31. Good thinking.

32. Marvelous
33. Exactly right!
34. SUPER1
35. Nice going!
36. You make it look easy.
37. Way to go.
38. Superb!!
39. You're getting better every day.

40. WONDERFUL!
41. I knew you could do it
42. Keep working on it, your getting better!
43. You're doing beautifully.
44. You're really working hard today
45. That's the way to do it.

46. Keep on trying.
47. That's it

51. I'm very proud of you.
52. You certainly did well today.
53. That's good.
54. I'm happy to see you working like that
55. I'm proud of the way you worked today.
56. That's the right way to do it
57. You're really learning a lot
58. That's better than ever.
59. That's quite an improvement
60. That kind of work makes me very happy.
61. Now you've figured it out
76. SENSATIONAL!!
77. That's the best ever.
78. Good remembering.
79. You haven't missed a thing.
80. You really make my job fun.
81. You must have been practicing.
88. SUPERIOR!
89. Good thinking.
90. Clever.

48. You've got it made.
49. You're very good at that
50. You're learning fast.
62. PERFECT!
63. FINE!!!
64. That's IT!
65. You figured that out fast
66. You remembered.
67. You're really improving.
68. I think you've got it now.
69. Well look at you go.
70. TREMENDOUS!
71. OUTSTANDING!
72. No that's what I call a fine job.
73. You did that very well.
74. That was first-class work.
75. Right on.

82. You got it made.
83. Good show.
84. CONGRATULATIONS!
85. Not bad.
86. Nice going (name of student)
87. OUTSTANDING!

91. Perfect.
92. Keep up the good work.

Table 13.1 provides some ways in which parents and teachers may promote academic and social growth, as well as raising the self-esteem of children. Table 13.1 shows 92 ways for saying to children that they have done a good job. These words and phrases are designed to reinforce good work habits and develop skills needed for academic and social success. Data in Table 13.1 is in concert with principles advocated by Bandura (1977). Bandura's social learning theory advocates how social learning may aid parents in using parental skills to remediate inappropriate behaviors.

Bandura proposed a very comprehensive and powerful social learning theory of modeling. Bandura's theory stands as the most popular theory of modeling today. One reason his theory is so popular is that it explicitly recognized that children imitate only a small fraction of all the responses they learn through observation. According to Bandura, children learn a multitude of brand new social responses simply by observing the actions of significant and salient models around them, including their parents, siblings, teachers, and playmates. Bandura calls this process observational learning and believes that this is a major way children acquire new patterns of social behavior. This theory fits into what most developmental psychologist say: that from 0-7 children are learning from significant others, and from seven to early teenage years they are modeling and demonstrating whey they have learned from others. During the teenage years, when children are looking for their own identity, they are looking to their friends and others in the same developmental stage for learning. If parents use their skills surrounding discipline and rewards during formative years, they still will be able to lovingly guide their children to adulthood without serious irreversible traumatic experiences. On the other hand, without parents employing good parenting skills, children may develop unacceptable social skills (Taylor, 1998).

Social learning theory implies that children learn from instruction and discipline they directly experience at the hands of their parents, teachers, and other socializing agents. Parents must give instruction to their children, establish routines, and serve as role models until their children have developed acceptable behaviors. Parents must decide when it is appropriate to transfer the locus of control from themselves to their children. Before transfer occurs, parents should be sure that their children have shown appropriate self-directed strategies to make independent decisions and to act appropriately on their own (Coleman, 1986). Parents will also need to be apprised of principles of child development and involved in in-service training relevant to classroom management strategies.

Techniques for Improving Parental Involvement

Parental involvement is a widely accepted practice among teachers. Parents can serve as partners to the teacher in the child's academic program. Henderson (1998) summed up the importance of parental involvement in the schools by stating that parents are a school's best friend. She listed several statements which have major implications for involving parents in the school: 1) The immediate family, not the school, provides the first instruction for the child; 2) Parental involvement in their children's education improves the chances for later academic and social success; 3) Parental involvement is most effective when it is comprehensively planned; 4) The earlier parents become involved in their children's education, the more likely they will be involved throughout the child's academic career.

It is incumbent upon the school to understand and appreciate the importance of parental and families' involvement in order to improve family/school cooperation. Significant benefits can be derived from involving parents early, not only when teachers encounter serious behavior problems from children. This can be accomplished by teachers forming positive relationships with parents. Formation of this relationship can assist teachers in dealing with inappropriate behavior. Positive relationships also improve communication and collaboration between teachers and parents.

It was commonly thought that parental involvement should be its strongest in the early school years, where strong foundations can be established. This view is expressed by many educators. Educators also support parental involvement and collaboration at the middle and secondary levels. Research tends to support that parental support is cumulative and the earlier parents are involved, the more successful the school experiences are (White & White, 1992; Finn, 1998; Epstein, 1995; Davies, 1996; Swick & Broadway, 1997).

To be effective, must be launched on two fronts, the home and school. Involving parents with their children's education at home augments the process, providing that strategies are collaboratively addressed by both teachers and parents. Achievement and managing classroom behavior of students tends to accelerate when both teachers and parents agree on common goals and objectives to be achieved. Parents can be instructed to focus on pro social skills and specific objectives which nurture them. (Specific guidelines are listed in Appendix G that parents may employ.)

All children benefit when parents are involved in the school. The education level of parents should not be a prerequisite for involving them in the school. There are many nonacademic tasks that parents can perform. All children are pleased and proud to see their parents involved in the school (Wang et al., 1993 Floyd, 1998; Clark, 1993; Wang et al., 1996).

Both the home and the school have a significant impact on students' behavior and attitudes. They are mostly formed at home during the early years and are reinforced by the parents as the child matures. If attitudes and behaviors are not reinforced by the school, negative ones may surface and impede the achievement of students (Taylor, 2000).

Development of School Policy

Parental involvement in school discipline policy is essential if the school is to have an effective behavior managing program. Parent should serve on all the major policy making bodies in the school concerned with developing the program. Parental involvement appears most effective when parents are directly involved. This has a direct impact on their children's behaviors. Parents can be effective when teachers define the conditions under which they serve. Specific ways should be articulated how parents can participate and collaborate in the program. Some in-service training may be needed by parents to effectively participate in the program (Thompson, 1998; Miller, 1998; Potter, 1996; Ohlrich, 1996). Brandt (1998) wrote that schools cannot meet the challenges of behavioral reforms without first doing a better job of connecting with parents and the communities in which they live.

In order to bring about effective changes and reforms in education, views and perceptions of parents must be an essential part of the formula. Parental input cannot be ignored.

Strategies recommended by the Commission of States (1996a) appear to be noteworthy of considering:
1. Listen to people first, talk later;
2. Expect to fail if you do not communicate well;
3. Make involving parents and the community a top priority;
4. Be clear about what it means to set high standards for all students, and what it will take to achieve them;
5. Show how new ideas enhance, rather than replace, the old ones;
6. Educate parents about the choices available to them; and
7. Help parents and other community members understand how students are assessed and what the results mean.

These authenticity strategies are essential in promoting trust between teachers and parents. Implementing these strategies will assist in reducing parents from all levels complaining about educators talking down to them (Commission of the States, 1996b). Over the last several decades, the school has had a difficult time in establishing effective partnerships with parents. Much of the fragmentation has occurred because of noninvolvement, hostility, or parental indifference towards the school. Many schools serving parents of children consider them a nuisance, unproductive, uneducated, lacking social graces, and not well-informed on education and social issues. Teachers should not conclude that those parents do not care for their children if they display the above traits. Nearly all parents are concerned with the welfare of their children. The relationship is further strained when parents internalize negative behaviors displayed by the school. They frequently view the school as an unacceptable place, which has no interest in them as individuals. There must be a total shift in this paradigm. The school must accept these parents and provide training in parenting skills. Parents may also reinforce the academic and social skills taught at school by teaching them at home. Parental influence can have a significant impact on children's behavior. This interaction is reciprocal and denotes how teachers view parental intervention strategies for dealing with inappropriate behavior.

Effective parental involvement programs acknowledge the fact that parents are a child's earliest and most influential teachers. Attempting to educate the child without parental support is a kin to trying to rake leaves in a high wind. Effective strategies, as outlined throughout this text, must be implemented to promote shared
responsibility for developing and implementing a discipline program (see Appendix J).

Collaborative Efforts at School

The National Association for the Education of Young Children (NAEYC, 2002) has advocated programs to develop closer support between parents and teachers. Behavioral goals should be developed in collaboration with parents. Parents should be equal partners in the formulating, implementing, and evaluating the effectiveness of a discipline programs for their children. It is commonly recognized today by the school that parental involvement is a necessary ingredient in planning any behavior program for their children.

In order to improve parental involvement into discipline programs, teachers should share responsibility through collaborative activities (Taylor, 2000). The following provisions are recommended:

1. Discipline programs serve parents, not children alone. All

policies should consider the impact they have on the parents as well as incorporating information from parents and direct involvement of them.

2. Discipline program practices in relating to parents must be in tune with widespread demographic changes, especially the characteristics and circumstances of parents being served by the program. The cultural values, lifestyles, and customs of the parents must be considered, respected, understood, and carefully integrated within the program. Some may have had unpleasant school experiences and may have concluded that their children are having similar experiences, thus reacting toward the teacher in a negative manner. Under these conditions it is incumbent that the teacher work to reduce those negative tones and attempt to develop positive relationships.

3. Parent and teacher confidence in each other provide foundation for healthy relationships. Strategies must be implemented to promote a collaborative reward system for children at home and school. Home rewards may include going to the movies, special treats, extra time to watch television when tastes have been successfully completed. Parents should be assured the reward system developed meets the needs and interest of their children, as well as promoting self-directed behaviors. Teachers should be assured by parents that they are using appropriate strategies to reinforce positive behavior. Some in-service training for parents may be needed to be conducted by the teacher.

4. Relationship with parents should be individualized in a way that inform parents of some positive behaviors displayed by their children ways of reporting positive behaviors or children should be clearly articulated by teacher to parents. Parents and teacher should agree about the types of rewards to be given to children. These rewards should serve as a source of motivating children to display appropriate behaviors.

5. Discipline programs should actively acknowledge parents as persons. The dignity of all persons should be respected, regardless of class, income, education, or racial or cultural values. The interests and needs of parents must be considered in any program in order to establish a quality discipline program at school.

6. Parent beliefs may be as important as basic support for facilitating parent participation in meetings and other activities. Parents should be encouraged to participate in meetings. Their

suggestions and recommendations should be considered in making decisions relevant to the behavioral program.

7. Definitions and assessment of the quality of the program should give greater attention to parents' perspectives and to the program practices with parents and families. Parents have seldom been involved in defining and evaluating the scope of programs. They have valuable input to give and must be permitted to share their views. It is important that these views be reflected in programs.

8. Professional education and credentials of teachers should promote skills in relating to parents. Part of the certification of teachers should be competencies required for effective work with parents. Innovative strategies should be in place to increase parental involvement in the school. Children are delighted when they see their parent involved in the school and behavior problems are diminished.

Tactics for Improving Colloborative Effort

Some recommended tactics for improving parental involvement and collaboration in classroom management have been educated by Giannetii and Sagarese (1997-98). They include:

1. Developing strategies for making parents more welcome in the school by inviting them to share their expertise with the classroom, hosting ethnic lunches, serving as chaperons, and tutoring children in academic subjects.

2. Advertising your expertise by letting parents know that you are competent in your designated areas.

3. Implementing an early warning system to inform parents of possible problems that children may encounter and provide strategies for correcting problems or performance before the children fail.

4. Accenting positive behaviors of the child rather than negative behaviors when reporting or conferring with parents.

5. Finding a common group to converse with parents by using their ethnic, religious, and cultural values.

6. Providing a safe environment by reassuring parents that their children will be safe in the classroom. Show parents some strategies that may be employed to protect their children.

7. Sharing with parents information that their children demonstrate in the classroom. Compare behaviors shown at home with school, such as information in anecdotal records.

8. Showing empathy, not sympathy, to parents. Empathy can assist the parents in dealing realistically with the problem, whereas sympathy appears to compound the negative aspect of the problem.

9. Being an effective and fair disciplinarian by applying the consequences of behavior equally to all who disregard the established rules.
10. Being a consistent role model that children can imitate and model.
The National PTA Standards and the aforementioned tactics can be effectively used in planning a supportive collaborative program. These tactics can easily be employed with parents with disabilities with little or few modifications.

Collaborative Problem-Solving Techniques

Collaborating with parents is a continuous process. There are several structures where effective collaborative strategies may be conducted, such as problem-solving groups and discussion groups. Most behaviors problems can be effectively addressed in conference settings (Kines, 1999; Wilson, 1997; McLaughlin, 1987; Graves; 1996; Steward, 1996).

Problem-Solving Groups

Parents who have similar behavioral problems related to their children may form groups to address them. These groups should be designed to discuss and recommend strategies for solving discipline problems in the classroom. Some possible strategies may be that:
1. The teacher allows additional time to complete tasks,
2. The child be placed in a different group or structure;
3. Additional services be provided;
4. Special instructional procedures be implemented;
5. Rewards are given for completing homework;
6. A quiet place be provided for the child to study;
7. Social skills development be enforced at home;
8. Appropriate physical and human resources to identified and used (Taylor, 2000).

Implementing these strategies will reduce the number of discipline problems in a classroom by recognizing some of the individual needs of the children. A creative teacher can infuse these strategies in his/her instructional program as the need arises.

The Problem-Solving Conference

The problem-solving conference is a technique that teachers and parents can use collaboratively to solve behavioral problems of children once rapport has been established. It may be necessary for the teacher to provide some training to the parent before initiating the conference (Mills & Bulach, 1996; Taylor, 2000). These conferences should clearly indicate specific behaviors that should be addressed, as well as the types of environment where the behavior is occurring, such as school, home, the community or in several places.

Guideline for Conduct Problem-Solving Conferences

1. Describe the behavior in objective and measurable teams.
2. Outline strategies to be used to reinforce behaviors.
3. Promote the use of all available information, including information from the home.
4. Agee that parents have equal rights to determine the   type and nature of the behavioral strategies to be employed.
5. Approval of the plan requires that parents endorse it.
6. A commonly agreed system for assessing behaviors should be intact.

Marsh (1999) summarized some of the values of collaborative relationships between teachers and parents.

1. School climate and programs;
2. Family support services;
3. Parents skills and leaderships;
4. Family and community relationships;
5. Teacher effectiveness.

Collaborative Planning

Research by Thompson (1998) clearly indicated that gaining professional support for the school involves developing strategies that incorporate widespread participation involving parents.

Parental leadership skill workshops should be instituted to enable parents to become active participants in developing behavioral standards. Before enacting standards, parents should be informed and given their endorsements. The school must show concern and respect for all participants regardless of class, education, or diversity (Davies, 1996). This approach assures that democratic views and values are considered.

Collaborative planning should be more than mere discussions and suggestions given by parents. Rather, they should be engaged in developing strategies to bring about improved classroom management techniques. Research findings tend to support that home to school collaboration is essential to the academic and social success of students. Collaborative arrangements increase parental decision-making and provide opportunities for school personnel to support parents in assisting their children to behave appropriately. Parents who have a conceptual understanding of the causes of behavioral problems can better assist the child and augment the teacher's behavioral program (Whiteford, 1998; Wolf, 1998).

A unique way for improving parent/teacher collaboration is to develop teams consisting of both parents and teachers. Miller (1998) offered the following suggestions for improving parents/teacher teams:

1. Be in touch long before the conference;
2. Be direct and personal in arranging the conference;
3. Be accommodating and try not to take no for an answer. Be flexible in setting meeting times around parents schedules;
4. Be on time;
5. Be prepared with handouts and work samples;
6. Be specific about problems;
7. Be knowledgeable as a team about each student;
8. Be welcoming;
9. Be in charge;
10. Be supportive;
11. Consider student-led conferences, which can be very effective for positive home-school relations;
12. Follow-up. Hold a team meeting to develop strategies for following up recommendations from the team; assign duties and responsibilities.

Team interaction is important and essential for improving the behavioral problems of children. This interaction can better assist the teacher and parent in understanding the strengths and weaknesses of the child and to plan appropriate behavior intervention (Taylor, 2000). The teacher may use one of the models discussed in Chapters 3 – 11 or abstract from several models.

Summary

Parenting is the process that develops skills needed for children to be successful in their environments. In order for parenting skills to be successful, parents need to be cognizant of techniques to employ, involving trust, respect, love, discipline, and communication. The recommended parenting skills for parents to use in directing and guiding their children have been developed premised upon the aforementioned techniques (Naeef, 1997; Dunst, Trivette, & Hamby, 1990; Powell, 1998; Leung, 1998).

Parents believe that they naturally know how to raise their children but, unfortunately, humans are not born preprogrammed with those child-rearing skills that will naturally help them to accurately discriminate and discern what to do when they confront a two-year-old's no's, or a seven-year-old's defiance about doing his or her homework, or a teenager's rebelliousness about obeying curfew set by the city to protect him or her from physical harm.

Parenting skills are not taught. Parents learn these skills through trial and error, strategies from their parents, information from published sources, and from specialists in the field. Parents generally use information from these sources to guide and direct the activities of their children. Most social scientists agree that parenting is a complex and dynamic process (Giannetti & Sagarese, 1997).

Parental involvement has been proven to be highly correlated with students demonstrating appropriate behavior in the classroom. Research findings have shown that differences in children's performance could be directly attributed to specific parental behaviors and interventions (Taylor, 2000). High achieving students usually have parents who constantly interact with the school and teacher, provide emotional support to their children, and are actively involved in homework (Wang, Haertel, &Walberg, 1993; Masten, 1994, Astone & Lanahan, 1998; Taylor, 1997; 1998). The reader should also refer to the various disciplines models discussed in the text for additional strategies to promote parental involvement. Parents must be directly involved in developing a behavioral management plan for their children. They should be equal partners in planning behavioral strategies. In-service training for parents should be provided to assist parents is understanding child development, causes of behavior problems, behavior intervention strategies as other problems as they relate to the uniqueness of each child. Through collaborative arrangements between teachers and parent, as articulated throughout this chapter, most inappropriate behaviors in the classroom can be significantly reduced or eliminated.

Classroom management techniques employed by teachers should be made known to parents. Parents should have an opportunity to observe children in the classroom. They should plan with the teacher strategies for improving on modifying the behavior. It is essential that the teacher accent the positive behaviors of children and encourage the parents to reinforce those behaviors of home (Taylor, 2000).

Chapter 14

Summary/Concluding Remarks

George R. Taylor

Factors Associated with Behavior Problems

We have adequately summarized factors associated with behavior problems in Chapter 1. Many of the problems are outside of the scope of the school to solve. Both home and community support are needed. Factors include but are not limited to the physical, social and culture traits at children. There are multiple cause of inappropriate behavior. Sapphire (1999) and Taylor (1998) wrote that public schools are mandated to educate every child within its boundaries, including immigrant and foster children, those who have disabilities, neglected, under nourished, and impoverished children, those from broken homes, and children from homes where they are abused. Educators must be cognizant of behavior problems associated with the aforementioned, and know how to choose the most appropriate intervention strategies, as outlined in Chapters 8 – 10.

We are cognizant of the fact that many behavior problems that cannot be adequately addressed or controlled by teachers, such as problems associated with psychological or biological factors. These problems demand the assistance of professionals. Teachers should make appropriate referrals as needed. Problems which are social cultural in nature will need the combined support of parents and community. Parents and community can provide both human and physical resources. These human and physical resources supplied by parents and community agencies can do much to reduce, minimize or eradicate behavior problems in the classroom (Taylor, 2000; Jones & Jones, 2000).

Behavior Problems Associated with Developmental Problems

As outlined in Chapter 1, many causes of behavior problems have their beginning with developmental problems. These problems usually begin in early childhood and if not corrected, could have severe replications for future types of inappropriate behaviors displayed by children. It is of prime importance that educators recognize these behaviors and intervene as early as possible, with the necessary human and physical resources to correct the behaviors (Lazarus, Davidson, & Pollefka, 1965).

Developmental Problems

Significant behavior problems may manifest themselves into many categories, however, principally they fall under academic failure, aggression, depression, and interpersonal problems with peers. Children who fail to acquire basic academic skills in the early grades are often rejected by their peers and are candidates for social and economic difficulties. Academic failure is usually associated with a variety of behavior problems, such as withdrawing from social activities, showing signs of aggression, frustration, and depression. Direct intervention by the teacher is highly recommended to change behaviors associated with developmental problems. Teachers may need to employ the assistant of mental health specialists for extreme cases of maladaptive behaviors (Kameenui & Simmons, 1990; Walker & Colvin, 1995; Kaslow & Rehm, 1991; Kauffman et al., 1991, 1998).

Providing Support to Teacher

Several techniques for providing support to teachers are depleted throughout the professional literature. The use of faculty study groups to suggest solutions to discipline problems have been widely used. These groups observe each other classrooms and meeting in teams to make specific recommendations for changes (Varner, 1999). Individual teacher's names are not used. Teacher consultant teams have been used to solve a variety of behavior problems. The team represents different levels of experiences, teaching assignments, and teaching styles. A coordinator is appointed to oversee the activities, completing paperwork, serving as the contact person and coordinating the problem solving process (Bauwens & Hourcade, 1995).

Collaborative Teaching Strategies

Collaborative teaching support teachers in several ways such as team teaching, complementary teaching, and support learning activities. These collaborative teaching strategies may take place individually or in groups. Support teams are divided into groups, based upon their competencies. All of the strategies are designed to give support to the teacher in solving behavior problems. Team teaching involves two or more teachers alternating and teaching lessons, the team usually consists of a regular and special education teacher. In complementary teaching the regular teacher is the primary teacher, the special education teacher provides support when needed. The special educator is the primary person to provide activities, skill practices are provided by the regular (Martin & Pear, 1992).

Raising One's Tolerance Level

Some teachers may find that by raising their tolerance levels, they are able to accept some behaviors that they would not normally accept. Some behaviors may conflict with personal beliefs, but they may be harmless, such as wearing one's pants below the belt, or by a child responding in a manner to what the teacher consider to be negative with practice a teacher may learn to accept such behaviors by raising his/her tolerance level. In support of the above, Long (1991) contended that when teachers demonstrate a willingness to make self-changes to improve the learning environments, they may significantly reduce potential behavior problems from emerging.

Teachers must assess what behaviors they are going to ignore or tolerate. By not making this judgment, teachers may become involved in simple conflicts which could have been resolved (Kauffman, Mostert, Trent & Hallahan, 1998). All behaviors should not be ignored or tolerated. Behaviors which constitute a risk to the child or others should not be ignored, but addressed with strategies and interventions outlines in this text.

Frequently, some behavior problems are outside of the scope of teacher's intervention. In some instances professional services must be sought to reduce, minimize or eradicate the problem. The role of parental and community support and resources should also be used to assist the teacher in providing support to assist students in controlling their behaviors. See Chapters 11 – 13 for specific strategies to employ.

Providing Support to Students

Discipline conferences with students have proven to be effective in reducing behavior problems. Students are requested to explain events responsible for the inappropriate behaviors, and to suggest ways for correcting them. This procedure also assist students in improving their reading, thinking, and speaking skills (Varner, 1999).

Problem Solving Strategies

Problem solving techniques employed by teachers can do much to reduce behavior problems in the classroom. When children are given the opportunity to explain their behaviors to teachers, they will feel free to express themselves, this creating an environment of trust and respect.

Once a climate of trust has been established, appropriate social skills can be taught to reduce to minimize inappropriate behaviors (Mountrose, 1999).

Managing classroom behavior is a complex task requiring self-questioning and careful reflections that even the best teacher must work to acquire and maintain (Kauffman, Mostert, Trent , & Hallahan, 1998), as reflect in discipline models discussed in Chapters 3 – 10. An effective teacher is one who can employ a variety of behavior management skills in his/her instructional program. When behavior problems surface in the classroom, teacher should go the source of the problems by trying to identifying them. Problems may range from 1) an inappropriate instructional program, 2) expectations and consequences of behaviors, 3) not raising one's tolerance level, 4) not determining problems associated with developmental problems and 5) not knowing what problem solving techniques to employ.

Inappropriate Instruction

The types of instructional demands made upon students may contribute to behavior problems. Teaching methods may not be relevant to the student. Tasks may not appeal to the interest or motivation levels of students (Taylor, 1999). Too much group instruction may be used when compared with individual instruction. The selection of teaching methods may not be matched with the abilities and learning styles of the children. Sufficient time allocated to academic tasks may not be present.

Sometimes teachers have no choice in the selection of teaching methods or strategies, they may be mandated by the local or state school districts when teachers to have flexibility to select teaching methods or strategies they should select these methods and strategies which appear to promote learning. To ensure that instruction is appropriate for children (Kauffman, Mostert, Trent & Hallahan , 1995) stated that teachers should reflect on the following questions.

1.   How relevant is the curriculum to the student?
2.   Do I have the option of teaching more relevant and functional information?
3.   To what extent could I have individualize instruction?
4.   How successful is the student performing in the curriculum?
5.   Am I using an approach to teaching that provides little structure, direction, positive feedback, or two much criticism?

6. How frequently do student have to respond to academic tasks?
7. What percentage of the time are students actually engaged in learning?
8. How much could I change the teaching strategies I use?

When teachers begin to address the listed questions, they may use a variety of strategies infused with the instructional program to remediate or correct inappropriate behaviors in the classroom.

Modeling Verbal and Non Verbal Skills

Effective teachers model verbal and non verbal skills. These skills are essential in communication (Kauffman, Mostert, Trent, & Hallahan, 1998). Appropriate communication skills can reduce many types of inappropriate behaviors from occurring verbal and non verbal communication skills include:

1. *Active Listening Skills.* These skills require that the teacher give the student his/her full attention and attempt to separate the emotional from the intellectual content. The process also provides the student with an opportunity to express why certain inappropriate behavior occurred.

    Teachers may use this information to plan behavior intervention for the student.

2. *Personal Proximity.* Close proximity to a student while talking may be interpreted as threatening, while standing too far may be misinterpreted as disinterest. Teachers must determine the personal space needed for each child. Some children will need more space than other. Hostile and aggressive students may need more space then others. Teachers should also be aware of limitations imposed by various cultures to proximity.

3. *Speaking Body Language.* Body language communicates interest or lack of interest during conversation. Individuals may interpret body language and posture as supportive or not supportive. Teachers should be aware that body language is frequently related or associated with cultures and may deviate within the same culture. When communicating with students from different cultures, the teacher should attempt to use body language and posture familiar to the student.

4. *Establishing Eye Contact and Facial Expressions.* Eye contact and facial expressions can assist in interpreting what one is thinking during conversation. Teachers should strive to match their expressions to the conversation under discussion . Eye contact and facial expressions can display a sense of interest or

disinterest. Prolong disapproving expressions can be distracting to the student. The teacher should be aware of cultural expectations when using and interpreting eye contact and facial expressions.

5. *Choosing Work Carefully.* When reflecting events leading up to describing a behavior, teachers should use words familiar to the students. Short statements are usually better than long ones. Some words denote different meanings in different languages. In essence, some words may do appropriately understood in one language, but inappropriate in others. It is incumbent upon teachers to know his/her audience and not to use language offensive to them.

6. *Pacing the Conversation.* When addressing a student about his/her behavior, teachers should be calm and speak slowly enough so that they are clearly communicating to the student. Do not speak to slowly or fast but pace your speaking. Be sure that you are not angry or frustrated. If so, postpone the conversation. Use your best voice and vary your volume. By varying your volume it will assist the student in focusing on the conversation.

7. *The Use of Questions.* Question properly posed to students will aid the teacher in assessing the reason for the behavior, as well as ways and types of interventions needed for correction. Questions may assist students in organizing their thoughts relevant to explain events responsible for the behavior. Questions may be posed as closed or open ended. Close questions are direct or specific and usually require a yes or no response. Open questions are not as restricted. They permit students to construct their own answers. Students must organize and think clearly before they respond.

Developing an environment where students feel free to talk about their behaviors is one of the greatest challenges of teaching. Communication skills must be developed which recognizes cultural differences. It is important that teachers understand the differences from the language students use at home and classroom language (Kauffman, Mostert, Trent, & Hallahan, 1998). The major goal of talking to students about the use of peer mediation strategies have proven to be successful in assisting students in internalizing their behaviors.

Peer Mediation Strategies

A success peer mediation program requires planning and preparation in order for it to be successful. Children must be taught early on how to perform the strategy. Techniques for problem solving should be infused within the curriculum and taught in the early grades. Mediation skills required of student mediators should be modeled by teachers. Children care what other children think of them. Positive peer pressure has proven to be a powerful deterrent in changing inappropriate behavior (Johnson, Johnson, Dudley, Wand, & Magnusion, 1995).

Solving problems through peer mediation has been proven to be a powerful, cost-effective process. The use of peer mediation strategies assist students in learning to listen to others and to consider other viewpoints. Peer mediation let students meet in a safe, supportive environment where they are not afraid of being honest to discuss their problems with peers (Taylor, 1998; Angaran and Beckwith, 1999) contended that through mediation, students learn communication skills that they can use in other situations. They learn to express their feelings into words, summarize what they hear and to develop empathy for others. Teacher expectations can promote or retard peer mediation strategies.

Expectations and Consequences of Behavior

Sometimes teachers do not clearly communicate to students what behaviors are expected. Students have little knowledge or how to demonstrate the behaviors. High expectations for some students may be too low for some children. Trying to determine the level of expectation requires that teachers be sensitive to the needs and abilities of pupils. Teachers should make sure that most students can successfully meet the expectations and that they are clearly communicated (Walker, Colvin, & Ramsey, 1995). When in doubt, teachers should model the expected behaviors. Children should be directly involved in selecting the consequences (Edwards, 1999).

Some students become frustrated because they can never measure upon to the teacher's expectations. The same can be said for teachers; they too become demoralized and began to doubt whether or not students can measure up to their expectations (Kauffman, Wong, Lloyd, Hung, & Pullen, 1991). In order to avoid this situation, teachers will have to develop a high degree of sensitivity to students traits and needs. In addition, teachers needed to review expectations and consequences to assess whether or not they:

1. Are justifiable with a rationale;
2. Consistently communicated expectation to students;
3. Biased against certain students; and

4.   Are required for everyone or exceptions made for certain individuals justified.

Providing Support to Parents

Parents need support in providing psycho-social and intellectual support to their children. Support should start while children are in the kindergarten and continue through senior high school. Depending upon the developmental level of the children, Friedland (1999) recommended the following steps:

1.   An orientation program starting in the kindergarten stressing developmental needs of children;
2.   Conducting five parental workshops at each grade level, emphasizing ways to meet the developmental needs of children at each level;
3.   Using parents as volunteers in the instructional program;
4.   The use of parents in community service and career internship program for secondary students; and
5.   Development of parent support teams for each grade level to assist in solving problems which may arise.

Parent Conferences

Parent conferences have proven to be an effective strategy for involving them in school. These conferences may take many forms such as by telephone, letters, e-mail, or face-to-face conferences. Face to face conferences appear to be the best approach, where issues and problems can be discussed openly and solutions mutually agreed upon. Parents can assist with field trips, work as resource individuals, tutor children, work as room mother, and work as paraprofessional are to name but a few involvement. Refer to Taylor 2000 for specific strategies.*

Strategies for Improving Discipline Problems

According to Vaner (1999) discipline is deceptive. It is not what ails chaotic classrooms; it is rarely a symptom of problems teachers have with instruction. Essentially when instruction is functional, realistic and based when the need and interest of children, behavior problems are reduced. Administrators can support teachers in improving instruction through systematic planning, classroom observations and providing physical and human resources.

1.

---

*G.R. Taylor (2000). Parental Involvement: A practical guide for collaboration and teamwork for students with disabilities. Springfield, IL: Charles C. Thomas.

Problems contributing to discipline problems may include the following:
1. Lack of preparing opening activities;
2. Teacher has not systematic discipline program in places;

3. Consequences of inappropriate behaviors are not well understood by children;
4. Children do not know how to complete assignments;
5. The instructional program is not realistic or functional for the children;
6. Teacher is not aware of differences in cultural behavioral patterns;
7. Psychological and biological causes of behaviors have not been assessed; and
8. Teachers receive little professional support from mental health specialists.

In selecting a discipline model, the following guidelines may be of benefit to teachers.

Selecting a Discipline Model

Chapters 8 – 10 summarizes some of the common discipline models in use today. In our opinion, teachers should draw from several models and develop a model which will address the needs and interest of his/her children. No one model is completely enough for teachers to use (Morris, 1996). The following guidelines are recommended.

Guideline 1

Choose from each model those strategies you believe are most likely to be used effectively in changing behavior problems in your class.

Guideline 2

Match strategies from each model with the nature and type of behavior problems, cognitive or behavioral displayed by students in your class. Infuse this information into intervention strategies.

Guideline 3

Adjust instructional strategies and techniques so that they are not contributing to behavior problems by making sure that information is relevant and functional to the student.

Guideline 4

Identify adequate physical and human resources to support the discipline model developed, including community resources and peer modeling

Guideline 5

Identify and assess problems associated with discipline

problems, such as poorly designed curriculum disabilities in children, poor parental involvement, poor environmental influences.

Guideline 6
Model appropriate behaviors for children to emulate and model.

Guideline 7
Provide opportunities for children to participate in developing rules and expectations employed in a classroom discipline plan.

Guideline 8
Teachers must be well trained and knowledgeable about classroom management theories, intervention and motivational strategies to improve behavior in the classroom.

Guideline 9
A democratic environment must be created where children participation is sough and valued in managing their classroom.

Guideline 10
A proactive approach should be used to reduce inappropriate behaviors in the classroom.

Implementing aforementioned guidelines will necessitate that teachers be apprised of the various strategies articulated throughout this text, as well as cooperatively use the expertise and competencies of school and community resources, a willingness to make self-changes to improve the learning environment, provide role models for students, and use developmental norms when designing discipline model.

Suggestions for Effective Classroom Management

A classroom that is managed effectively is necessary if desirable pupil learning is to occur. Prevention of difficulties rather than punishment for misbehavior is desirable. The use of the following suggestions will be valuable in establishing and maintaining effective management in the classroom.

Have a Good Program

Busy pupils are not troublemakers. Provide a program that interests, challenges, and satisfies pupils. Include activities that enable pupils to "let off stem" in acceptable ways.

Help Pupils Set Standards

Work cooperatively with the pupils to set up reasonable standards of behavior. State the standard positively. Post the standards.

Be Consistent

The good teacher is not mercurial. Children like to know what to expect.

Let Them All Help

Don't leave any child out with the room chores and responsibilities are assigned. A sense of belonging reduces discipline problems.

Divert Mischief-Makers

Invite disturbers of the peace to give some service to the class or to the school. Commend them for the service. Aggressive behavior may be an expression of hunger for attention.

Avoid Creating Discipline Problems

A classroom ruled by fear, threats, or unreasonable punishment creates
more problems than it solves.

Make Learning an Adventure

Boredom is a potent cause of discipline trouble. If your teaching is
interesting and exciting to you, it will be to your pupils too. Interest,
like enthusiasm and the measles, is contagious. Without interest, the
pupil learns little.

Don't Talk Too Much

Use posture, facial expressions, and silence to cut down on the need for
talking. Talking isn't necessarily teaching. The good teacher get his/her
pupils to talk and guides their discussion.

Don't Try to Talk Above Confusion

If what you say is worth saying, it's worth hearing. Keep your voice
down and refuse to talk about confusion. All children are entitled to
the kind of discipline that results in self-control, in emotional stability,
and in the moral and spiritual values that contribute to the self-concept.

Charting Frequency of Behaviors

Example 1:   Record the frequency of behaviors for obtaining baseline data (the number of times a behavior occurs before an intervention is initiated) and the effectiveness of the interventions.

Behavior Frequency Chart

Child's Name:_____Date:_____

Behavior:_____

Date	Activity	Time Interval	Number of Behavior

Use one color for baseline data and a different color to record the frequency of behaviors once you have started the intervention. It is best to use one chart for each activity. However, if you wish to record more than one activity on a chart, use a different color for each activity.

Example 2:   Record the frequency of behaviors for obtaining
                  baseline data (the number of times a behavior occurs
                  before an intervention is initiated) and the
                  effectiveness of the interventions.

Behavior Frequency Chart

Child's Name: _____   Date: _____

Behavior:_____

	Baseline Frequency			Frequency of Behaviors with Intervention								
30x												
F												
R 25x												
E												
Q 20x												
U												
E 15x												
N												
C 10x												
Y	2	3	4	1	2	3	4	5	6	7	8	etc.
				Day								

Teaching Routines

Most effective managers spend considerable time in the beginning of the year teaching routines. However, they do not teach these routines all at once. They begin by first teaching the routines that are absolutely necessary to run a classroom; then, using a piece-by-piece approach, new routines are added after the students are regularly mastering those expectations that have been established first.

Establishing management routines requires slow, regular, and consistent implementation, as indicated in the following guidelines:

1   Mentally walk through each routine to be sure that it is both efficient and possible for the ages of your students.

2.   Instruction:
      a.   Relate the new behaviors to previous ones and set expectations for new behavior (anticipatory set).
      b.   Teach new behaviors directly through structured activities

3.   Model:

      a.   Walk the students through the routines during the first few weeks.
      b.   Demonstrate the set of desired behaviors.

4.   Checking for understanding/guided practice

      a.   Be sure that the children understand the directions by asking them to restate them in their own terms.
      b.   Give directions for each step as students practice.
      c.   Provide for practice by...
- giving less frequent directions
- giving cues to start the routine
- having students orally repeat the "cue" directions, and
- having students repeat the directions

5.   Independent practice:

    a. Give students an opportunity to practice on their own
    b. Constantly monitor the use of the routine through
       observation
    c. Provide for reinforcement by evaluating the use of the
       routine with the students (provide both positive and
       negative feedback)

Suggestions Handling Unacceptable Classroom Behavior

Prevention is better than cure; therefore, look for signs, as children enter the classroom, that will alert you to possible outbreaks later on.

Below are listed some possible infractions of the regularly accepted rules and regulations that permit a well managed classroom. To the right are listed possible ways of handling the infractions

Means of Handling Incidents

Unacceptable Behavior	Immediate	Deferred
Yelling Out	Ignore	Explain reasons for not allowing this
	Teach Courtesy	Set up a system of giving rewards for remembering to follow rules.
	Encourage pupils to follow routine set up earlier.	
Hitting Another Child	Separate the two (physically or/and geographically).	Allow each child to explain what he/she thinks caused the behavior.
	Send a letter to parents if this is a reoccurring infraction.	With inductive questioning, help children decide how this behavior could have been avoided.

Unacceptable Behavior	Immediate	Deferred
	Send pupils involved to the office with a pass and a note.	
Making Loud Noises with Pens, Pencils, Books, Desks, Lips, etc.	Remove object that is being used from child without a word.	Encourage children to practice self-control.
	Put your fingers to your lips to remind child what he/she is disturbing others.	Encourage child to try to qualify for the "Good Citizenship Award."
	Move desk several inches away from other furniture.	
Defacing Property	Remove object that is being used from the child.	Discuss with child the difficulties involved and the expenses incurred in having school property repaired.
	Remind child what he/she is doing; he/she may be daydreaming; therefore, not consciously aware of his/her actions.	Initiate a clean-up campaign emphasizing "Pride in Our School."
	Provide change of pace activities at regular intervals during the school day.	Encourage child to qualify for the "Good Citizenship Award."
Calling Bad Names	Have pupil tell what the other child's name really is	Discuss self-respect and respect for others.
	Have pupil participate	Discuss reasons for

Unacceptable	Immediate	Deferred
Getting Out of Seat	Teachers should be observant at all times so that this incident can be stopped before it is carried through.	Redirect child's path toward the book case to get a specific book; to the cupboard to bring you something needed to pick up trash and put it in the trash container, etc.
	Be sure that all children are listening and following specific directions.	Send letter to parents asking for assistance in training child to develop self-control.
	Ask child if the teacher can help, as you walk toward him/her, showing your interest in whatever concerns him/her.	
	Have impromptu "change of pace" activities when children appear restless.	
Throwing Things Across the Room or Shooting Paper Balls with Rubber Bands	Caution child that such behavior cannot be accepted in the classroom.	Discuss with child his reasons for such behavior (in private).
	Cite possible dangers and confusion caused by such behavior.	Send letter to parent if this is a recurring act.

Positive Consequences that Work for All Grade Levels

We have found that teachers can always use effective consequences to motivate an individual student or an entire class. Here are a number of field-tested ideas for you to add to your list.

Elementary-Level Positive Consequences for Individual Students

> ➤ Smile-o-grams or happy grams or other positive notes sent to parents.
> ➤ Free time for good behavior
> ➤ Positive phone calls and progress reports
> ➤ Work as classroom aides
> ➤ Immediate rewards, treats, stars, stickers, etc.
> ➤ Lunch with teacher
> ➤ Citizen of the day or week
> ➤ Work with custodian or librarian
> ➤ Wear special button
> ➤ Take home classroom pet
> ➤ Special Chair
> ➤ Spotlight student's work
> ➤ Extra library time

Positive Consequences for the Entire Class

> ➤ Extra recess
> ➤ Popcorn party or other party
> ➤ Special principal visit
> ➤ Extra movies or cartoons
> ➤ Special lunch
> ➤ Cooking
> ➤ Extra free time
> ➤ Special arts and crafts
> ➤ Field trips

➤ Public recognition of group by principal
➤ Group photographers
➤ Extra physical education
➤ Special class visitor (fireman, magician)

Sample Class Rules

Primary
1. Follow directions.
2. Walk in the classroom.
3. Raise your hand and wait to be called on, unless given permission to do otherwise .
4. Keep your hands and feet to yourself.
    5. Return materials to the proper storage place when you are finished using them.
    6. Food, candy and gum are not allowed in class.
7. Receive permission and a pass before leaving the classroom.

Upper Elementary

1. Follow directions.
2. Be in your seat when the bell rings.
3. Have all appropriate materials and supplies at your desk , ready to begin work when the bell rings.
4. Receive permission and a pass before leaving the classroom
5. Keep hands, feet, and all objects to yourself.
6. Food, candy, and gum are not allowed in class.

Secondary

1. Follow directions.
2. No interruptions or personal remarks are permitted during classroom discussion.
3. Come to class with all materials.
4. Food, candy, and gum are not allowed in class.
5. Be in your assigned seat, ready to work when the bell rings.
6. Receive permission and a pass before leaving the classroom.

Procedures/Rules

Know the difference between procedures and rules.

Examples of Procedures

1. Stack textbooks on table B
2. Enter the room by door A.
3. Line up from the back first.
4. Wash paint brushes before storing them.

Examples of Rules

1. Follow directions.
2. Complete all assignments.
3. Do not leave the classroom without permission.
4. Work independently.

Twelve Guidelines to Good Discipline in the Home

1. Do It Yourself
    Discipline should not be transferred from one parent to the other. When a mother says to a child, "Wait till your father gets home; he will give it to you!" it's the same as saying "I am not able to discipline you, it is beyond my ability." This engenders lack of respect for the mother, makes the father into a bully, and fosters a bad family situation.

2. Try Voice Control
    Don't yell. How difficult this is, especially with adolescents! If you raise your voice and the child starts yelling back, it ends up as a yelling contest. Saying something loud does not make it any more convincing. Try calmness; it is good for your nerves. How's your sense of humor?

3. Open Person At A Time
    A child should not feel that everyone is "ganging up" on him. Whoever starts the corrective procedure should complete it without interference. A parent who does interfere makes it possible for the child to "play" his parents one against the other to his own advantage.

4. Kiss and Make Up
    But not in the Hollywood style. If the punishment has been just, there is no need for a great dramatic scene. After a severe punishment, one that a child knows he deserves, avoid a too emotional scene. It may fulfill a need for a parent, but children have been known to misbehave in order to get this type of attention from parents.

5. Keep Little Incidents Little
    There are some things that children do that are part of their growing up and part of a stage through which they are passing. A child cannot be good all the time. Minor wrong-doings should not be magnified to the proportion of a federal case. Once an incident is over/it should forgotten. Do not refer to it

unnecessarily. If you nag, the child will not listen. Relax; enjoy him!

6.   Be Firm and Decisive
       Children prefer parents who are just and firm. Firmness does not include hitting or slapping, for constant slapping becomes valueless. Discipline a child for endanger his life or that of others—but explain what the danger is. Firmness and decisiveness are effective parenting tools.

7.   Punishment Should Fit The Crime
       By punishment, we mean imposing a penalty. It may be mild or severe, depending on the misbehavior. A suitable penalty may be depriving a child of some favorite activity. Penalize a child who keeps violating his curfew hour by taking away those privileges—not his television of his weekly allowance. Keep the punishment reasonable in order to enforce it.

8.   Love, and Penalty of It
       A child is quick to sense his parent's feelings. Children need a great deal of love and affection, and the desire to please is one of the most powerful tools of discipline. Show displeasure with wrong conduct, but avoid saying, "I won't love you if...". A child must learn that he can't have everything he wants.

9.   Be Truthful And Keep Promises

       Children who are untruthful, may be imitating their parents. They are keen to notice how truthful you are in your dealings with them and with others. When you make a promise, keep it. Avoid retractions by saying, "We will see", when you do not wish to commit yourself. If you make a habit of bribing, you create a discipline problem.

10.   Be Persistent And Consistent
       Set up simple and realistic standards of behavior and stick to them. Children feel more secure if they know there is a limit to unseemly behavior. When a child begins to nag of cry to get his way, it's a temptation to let him to get rid of him. If this happens, he learns that, his parent is an easy mark and he'll take advantage of it.

11.   Accentuate The Positive
        Give a child a good reputation and he will live up to it. Pick out a
        child's good points and work on these. A word of praise and
        encouragement can. Be a good start.

12.   Make The Child Feel Trusted
        Treat the family as a unit. A child should feel that he, too, is part of
        the family. He responds accordingly if he shares your confidence,
        problems, and security. This does not mean that situations beyond
        his age should be discussed with him. Discuss only things which
        concern him, but make him feel that he is a trusted member of the
        family at all times.

Endnotes

1. George R. Taylor. (2001). Educational intervention and services for children with exceptionalities: Strategies and perspectives. Springfield, IL: Charles C. Thomas.
2. For specific research strategies in group processes refer to J. S. Kounin. (1970). Discipline and group management in classroom. New York: Rinehart and Winston
3. Kohn, A. (1996). Beyond discipline. Compliance to Community. Alexandra, VA: Association for Supervision and Curriculum Development.
4. Glasser, W. (1969). Schools without failure. New York: Harper and Row.
5. For specific examples of response types to Lee Canter and Marlene Canter. (1992). Assertive discipline. Santa Monica, CA: Lee Canter and Associates.
6. Dreikurs, R., Grunwald, R. B., & Pepper, F. C. (1982). Maintaining sanity in the classroom: Classroom management techniques (2nd ed.). New York: Harper and Row.
7. Arends, Richard. (2000). Learning to teach (5th ed.). Boston: McGraw Hill.
8. Taylor, George R. (1999). Curriculum models and strategies for educating individuals with disabilities in inclusive classrooms. Springfield, IL: Charles C. Thomas.
9. Taylor, George R. (2000). Parental involvement: A practical guide for collaboration and teamwork for students with disabilities.

Bibliography

Adger, C.T., Wolffam, W., & Detwylek, J. (1993). Language differences. A new approach for special educators. *Teaching Exceptional Children, 26* (1), 44-47.

Alberto, P.A., & Troutman, A.C. (1998). *Applied behavior analysis for teachers (4th ed.)* Upper Saddle River, N.J.: Prentice-Hall.

Algozzine, B., Ruhl, K., & Ramsey, R. (1991). *Behaviorally disordered. Assessment for identification and instruction.* Reston, VA: The Council for Exceptional Children.

Anderson R.J., & Decker, R. H. (1993). The principal's role in special education programming. *NASSP Bulletin 77* (550), 1-6.

Angaran, S. & Beckwith, K. (1999). Elementary school peer mediation. *The Education Digest, 65* (1), 23 – 25.

Arends, R.I. (2000). *Learning to teach.* Boston: McGraw Hill.

Armstrong, S.W., & McPherson, A. (1991). Homework as a critical component in social skills instruction. *Teaching Exceptional Children, 24*(1), 45-47.

Astone, N.M, & Lanahan, S.S. (1998). Family structure, parental practices, and high school completion. *American Sociology Review, 56*(3), 309–320.

Ayers, W. (1989). Childhood at risk. *Educational Leadership, 46,* 70 – 72.

Bandura, A. (1969). *Principles of behavior modification.* New York: Holt, Rinehart, and Winston, Inc.

Bandura, A. (1977). Self-efficacy toward a unifying theory of behavior change. *Psychological Review, 84,* 191-215.

Barker, R.G. (1968). *Ecological psychology.* Stanford, CA: Stanford University Press.

Barth, R. (1990). *Improving schools from within.* San Francisco: Jossey-Bass, Inc.

Bauwen, J., & Hourcade, J.J. (1995). *Cooperative teaching: Rebuilding the school house for all students.* Austin, TX: Pro-Ed.

Biehler, R. & Snowman., J. (1982). *Psychology applied to teaching.* Boston: Houghton Mifflin.

Bilken, D. (1989). Making a difference. Ordinary, I & W. Stainback & M. Forest (eds). *Educating all children in the mainstream of regular education.* Baltimore, MD Paul H. Brookes.

Brandt, R. (1998). Listen first. *Educational Leadership,* 55(8), 25-30.

Breen, M.J., & Fiedler, C.R. (1996). *Behavioral approaches to assessment of youth with emotional behavioral disorders.* Austin: ProEd.

Brendtro, L. & Long, N. (1995). Breaking the cycle of conflict. *Educational Leadership,* 52-56.

Brigge, M., & Hunt, M. (1968). *Psychological foundation of education* (2nd ed.) New York: Harper and Row.

Brophy, J., & Good, T. L. (1986). Teacher behavior and student achievement. In M. C. Witrock (Ed.). *Handbook on Research in Teaching* (3rd ed.). New York: Macmillan.

Butler, O.B. (1989). Early help for kids at risk: Our nation's best investment. NEA Today, 7, 51 – 53.

Caldwell, L. (1997). Tips to parents from your pre-schooler. *Child Care Information Exchange,* 113, 89.

Cangelosi, J.S. (1990). *Cooperation in the classroom: Students and teachers together* (2nd ed.). Washington, DC: National Educational Association.

Cangelosi, J.S. (2000). *Classroom management strategies: Gaining and maintaining students' cooperation.* New York: John Wiley & Sons, Inc.

Canter, L., & Canter, M. (1992). *Assertive discipline: Positive behavior management for today's classroom.* Santa Monica, CA: Canter and Associates.

Cazden, N.C.B. (1986). Class discourse. In M.C. Wittrock (Ed.), *Handbook on Research on Teaching* (3rd ed.). New York: MacMillan.

Charles, C.M. (1992). *Building classroom discipline: From models to practice* (4th ed.). New York: Longman.

Charney, R.S. (1992). *Teaching children to care: Management in the responsive classroom.* Greenfield, Mass: Northeast Foundation for Children.

Cheney, D., Barringer, C., Upham, D., & Manning, B. (1995). Project testing: A model for developing education support teams through interagency network for youth with emotional or behavioral disorders. *Special Services in the Schools,* 10 (2), 57-76.

Christopolos, F., & Valletutti, P. (1969). Defining behavior modification. *Educational Technology,* 9, 28.

Clark, R.M. (1993). Family life and school achievement. Chicago: University of Chicago Press.

Coleman, M.C. (1986). *Behavior disorders: Theory and practice.* Englewood Cliffs, NJ: The Free Press.

Colvin, G. (1992). *Managing acting-out behaviors.* Longmont, CO: Sopris West.

Colvin, G., Kameenui, E. J., & Sugia, G. (1993). Reconceptualizing behavior management and school-wide discipline in general education. *Education and Treatment of Children*, 16 (4), 361-381.

Colvin, G., Suagi, G., & Patching, B. (1998). Pre-correction: An instructional approach for managing predictable problem behavior. *Intervention in School and Clinic, 28*, 143 – 150.

Committee for Economic Development. (1987). *Children in need: Investment strategies for the educationally disadvantaged.* New York.

Cullingford, C. (1996). The reality of childhood. *Time Educational Supplement*, 4193, 15.

Cummings, C. (2000). *Winning strategies for classroom management.* Alexandria, VA: Association for Supervision and Curriculum Development.

Cummings, J. (1984). *Bilingual and special education: Issues in assessments pedagogy.* San Diego: College Hill Press.

Dalli, C. (1991). *Scripts for children's lives: What do parents and early childhood teachers contribute to children's understanding of events in their lives.* ERIC ED.344664.

Davies, D. (1996). Partnership for students success. *New Schools, New Communities, 12*(3), 14-21.

Deiro, J.A. (1996). *Teaching with heart: Making healthy connections with students.* Thousand Oaks, CA: Corwin Press, Inc.

Dewitt, P. (1994). The crucial early years. *Time Magazine, 143*, 16, 68.

Dinkmeyer, D. & Dinkmeyer, D., Jr. (1976) Logical consequences: A key to the reduction of disciplinary problems. *Phi Delta Kappan*, 57, 664-666.

Doyle, W. (1979). Classroom task and students' abilities. In P.L. Petson and H.J. Walbert (Eds.). *Research on teaching: Concepts, findings and implications.* Berkeley, CA: McCutchan.

Doyle, W. (1986). Classroom organization and management. In M.C. Wittrock (Ed.) *Handbook of Research on Teaching*. New York: MacMillan.

Doyle, W. & Carter, K. (1984). Academic tasks in classrooms. *Curriculum Inquiry, 14*, 129 – 149.

Dreikurs, R. (1960). *Fundamental of adlerian psychology*. Chicago. Alfred Adler Institute.

Dreikurs, R., & Grey, L. (1968). *A new approach to discipline: Logical consequences*. New York: Hawthorne Books.

Dreikurs, R. (1968*). Psychology in the classroom: A manual for teachers* (2nd ed.). New York: Harper & Row.

Dreikurs, R., & Cassel, P. (1972). *Discipline without tears*. New York: Hawthorne Books.

Dreikurs, R., Grunwold, B.B., & Pepper, F.C. (1982). *Maintaining sanity in the classroom: Classroom management techniques* (2nd ed.). New York: Harper & Row.

Dreikurs, R., Bronia, G.B., & Pepper, F.C. (1998). *Maintaining sanity in the classroom: Classroom management techniques* (2nd ed.). New York: Harper & Row.

Dunst, G.J., Trivette, C.M., Hamby, D., & Pollock, B. (1990). Family systems correlates the behavior of young children with handicaps. *Journal of Early Intervention, 14*(3), 204-218.

Education Commission of the States. (1996b). *Bending without breaking*. Denver, CO: Author.

Education Commission of the States. (1996b). *Listen, Discuss, and Act*. Denver, CO: Author.

Edwards, C.H. (1997). *Classroom discipline and management* Englewood Cliffs, NJ: Prentice Hall.

Edwards, C.H. (1997). *Classroom discipline and management* (2nd ed.). Upper Saddle River, NJ: Prentice Hall.

Epstein, J.J. (1995). School, family, community, partnerships: Caring for the children we share. *Phi Delta Kappan, 77*(9), 701-712.

Erikson, E.H. (1959). Identify and life cycle. *Psychological Issues*. Monograph, 1. New York: International Universities Press.

Eisner, E.H. (1991). What really counts in school? *Educational Leadership, 10*, 17.

Finn, J.D. (1998). Parental engagement that makes a difference. *Educational Leadership, 55*(8), 20-24.

Fisher, C.W., Berliner, D.C., Filby, N.N., Marliave, R., Cahen, L.S., & Dishaw, M.M. (1980). Teaching behaviors academic learning time, and student achievement: An overview, Inc. Denham and A. Lieberman (Eds.), *Time to Learn*. Washington, DC: National Institute of Education.

Floyd, L. (1998). Joining hands: A parental involvement program. *Urban Education, 33*, 123-125.

Forest, M. (1990). *Maps and cities*. Presentation at Peak Parent Center Workshop. Colorado Springs.

Friedland, S. (1999). Less violence? Change school culture. *The Education Digest,65* (1), 6 – 9.

Fuchs, D. Fuchs, L., Mathes, P., & Simmons, D. (1997). Peer-assisted learning strategies: Making classrooms more responsive to diversity. *American Educational Research Journal, 34* (1) 174 – 206.

Fulk, C.L. (1997). How to pinpoint and solve day-to-day problems. Teaching Exceptional Children, 29 (3), 55-59.

Giannetti, C., & Sagarese, M. (1992*). The roller-coaster years: Raising your child through the maddening yet magical middle school years*. New York: Broadway Books.

Ginott, H. (1971). *Teacher and child*. New York: MacMillan.

Ginott, H. (1973). Drive children sane. *Today's Education, 62*, 20 – 25.

Ginott, H. (1972). I am angry! I am appalled! I am furious! *Today's Education, 61*, 23 – 24.

Glasser, W. (1969). *School with failure*. New York: Harper Row.

Glasser, W. (1984). *Control theory: A new explanation of how we control our lives*. New York. Harper & Row.

Glasser, W. (1986). *Control theory in the classroom*. New York: Harper & Row.

Glasser, W. (1989). *Control theory in the practice of reality therapy: Case studies*. New York: Harper & Row.

Glasser, W. (1990). *The quality school*. New York: Harper & Row.

Gnagey, W. J. (1975). *Maintaining discipline in classroom instruction*. New York: Macmillan.

Goodall, K. (1972). Who's who and when in behavior shaping. *Psychology Today*, 6, 53-56.

Goodlad, J.L. (1984). *A place called school*. New York: McGraw-Hill

Gordon, T. (1974). *T.E.T.: Teacher effective training.* New York: Peter Hi Wyden.

Gordon, T. (1989*). Discipline that works: promoting self-discipline in children.* New York: Penguin.

Graves, D.H. (1996). Parent meetings: Are you ready? How you prepare matters most in talking about a child's writing. *Instructor, 105,* 42-43.

Haberman, M. (1994). Gentle teaching in a violent society. *Educational Horizons,* 131-135.

Hallahan, D.P., & Kauffman, J.M. (1997). *Exceptional learners: Introduction to special education* (7th ed.). Boston: Allyn & Bacon.

Hatch, T., & Gardner, H. (1988). How kids learn: What scientists say. New research on intelligence. *Learning,* 37.

Henderson, A.T. (1988). Parents are a school's best friend. Bloomington, IN: *Phi Delta Kappa,* 135.

Hudley, C., & Graham, S. (1995). School-based intervention for aggressive African-American boys. *Applied and Preventive Psychology, 4,* 185-195.

Jackson, J.T., & Owens, J.L. (1999). A stress management classroom. Tool for teacher of children with BD. *Intervention in school and clinic, 35* (2), 74-78.

Johnson, D.W., & Johnson, F.P., (1994*). Joining together: Group theory and group skills* (4th ed.) Englewood Cliffs, NJ: Prentice Hall.

Johnson, D., Johnson, R., Dudley, B., Wand, M., & Magnusion, D. (1995). The impact on peer mediation training on the management of school and home conflicts. *American Educational Research Journal, 32* (4), 829–844.

Jones, F.H. (1987a). *Positive classroom discipline.* New York: McGraw-Hill.

Jones, F.H. (1987b). *Positive classroom instruction.* New York: McGraw-Hill.

Jones, F. H. (1993). Assessing your classroom and school-wide student management plan. Beyond Behavior, 4 (3), 9-12.

Jones, F. H., & Jones, L.S. (1989). *Comprehensive classroom management, motivating and managing students.* Needham Heights, MA.: Allyn & Bacon

Jones, F.H.,& Jones, L.S. (2000). *Comprehensive classroom management, creating communities of support and solving problems.* Needham Heights, MA.: Allyn & Bacon

Kagan, S.L. (1989). Early core and education: Beyond the school house doors. *Phi Delta Kappan,* 107 – 112.

Kameenui, E.J., & Darch, C.B. (1995). *Instructional classroom management. A proactive approach to behavior management.* White Plains, New York: Logman.

Kameenui, E.J., & Simmons, D.C. (1990). Designing instructional strategies: The prevention of academic learning problems. Columbus, OH: Charles E. Merrill.

Kandel, C. (2000). When a student says, "No." *CEC Today,* 7(4), 12–14.

Kandel, M., & Kandel, E. (1994). Flights of memory. *Discover Magazine,* 32 – 38.

Kapos, K. (1995). Schools studying 220-day year. *Salt Lake Tribune,* 250 (36) B1 – B3.

Kaslow, N.J., & Rehm, L.P. (1991). Childhood depression. In T.R. Kratochwill & R.J. Morris (Eds.). *The Practice of Child Therapy* (2nd ed.) New York: Pergamon.

Katz L.G. (1991). *The teacher's role in social development of young children.* ERIC ED. 331642.

Kauffman, J.M. (1997). *Characteristics of emotional and behavior disorders of children and youth* (6th ed.). Uppersaddle River, N.J.: Prentice-Hall.

Kauffman, J.M., Lloyd, J.W., & McGee, K.A. (1989). Adaptive and maladaptive behavior: Teachers' attitudes and their technical assistance needs. *Journal of Special Education, 23,* 185-200.

Kauffman, J.M., Mostert, M.P., Trent, SC., & Hallahan, D. P. (1998). *Managing classroom behavior: A reflective case-based approach* (2nd ed.). Boston: Allyn and Bacon.

Kauffman, J.M., Wong, K.L.H., Lloyd, J.W., Hung, L., & Pullen, P.L. (1991). What puts pupils at risk? An analysis of classroom teachers' judgments of pupils' behavior. *Remedial and Special Education, 12* (5), 7 – 16.

Kazid, A. E. (1973). Issues in behavior modification: With mentally retarded persons. *American Journal of Mental Deficiency, 78,* 134.

Kessler, J.W.C. (1966). *Psychology of childhood.* New Jersey: Prentice Hall.

Kerr, M.M. & Nelson, C.M. (1998). *Strategies for managing behavior problems in the classroom* (3rd ed.). Upper Saddle River, NJ: Prentice-Hall.

Kines, B. (1999). The parent connection. *Teaching K-8, 6*(4), 33.

Kohn, A. (1993). *Punished by reward*. Boston: Houghton Mifflin.

Kohn, A. (1996). *Beyond discipline: Compliance by community.* Alexandria, VA: Association for Supervision and Curriculum Development.

Kounin, J.S. (1970a). *Discipline and group management in classrooms*. New York: Holt, Rinehart & Winston

Kounin, J.S. (1970b). Observing and delineating techniques at managing behavior in classrooms. *Journal of Research and Development in Education, 4* (1), 62-72.

Kounin, J. S., Grump, P. V., & Ryan, J. S. III. (1961). Explorations in classroom management. *Journal of Teacher Education, 12,* 235-247.

Krasner, L., & Ullman, L.P. (1965). *Research in behavior modification*. New York: Holt, Rinehart, & Winston.

Lazarus, A.A., Davidson, G.C., & Pollefka, D.A. (1965). Classical and operant factors in the treatment of school phobia. *Journal of Abnormal Psychology, 70,* 225-229.

Leung, K. (1998). Parenting styles and academic achievement: A cross-cultural study. *Merrill-Palmer Quarterly, 44*(2), 157-172.

Lewis, C., Schaps, E., & Watson, M. (1996). "The caring classroom's academic edge." *Educational Leadership, 54* (1), 15-21.

Lippitt, R., & White, R. (1958)/ An experimental study of leadership and group life. In E.E. Macoby, T.M. Newcomb, and F.L. Hartley (Eds.). *Readings in Social Psychology.* New York: Holt, Rinehurt & Winston.

Long, J.D. (1991). Self-assessment: A first step toward more effective classroom management. *Contemporary Education, 62* (3), 174 – 176.

Lovitt, T. (1970). Behavior modification: The current science. *Exceptional Children,* 38, 58-91.

Macht, J. (1990). *Managing classroom behavior: An ecological approach to academic and social learning.* New York: Longman.

MacMillian, D., & Forness, S.R. (1970). The origins of behavior modification with exceptional children. *Exceptional Children, 37*, 93-100.

MacNaughton, R.H. & Johns, F.A. (1991). Developing a successful schoolwide discipline program. *NASSP Bulletin, 75* (536), 47 – 57.

Martin, G. & Pear, J. (1992). *Behavior modification* (4th ed.). Englewood Cliffs, NJ: Prentice Hall.

Marsh, D. (1997). Yearbook: *Preparing out schools for the 21st century.* Alexandria, VA: Association for Supervision and Curriculum Development.

Marshall, H.H. (1987). Motivational strategies of three fifth-grade teachers. *Elementary School Journal, 88*, 135-150.

Masten, A. (1994). Resilience in individual development: Successful adaptation despite risk and adversity. In M.C. Wang & E.W. Gordon (Eds.) *Educational Resilence in Inner-City American.* Hillsdale, NJ: Erlbaum.

Matsueda, R.L., & Heimer, K. (1987). Race, family, structure, and delinquency: a test differential association and social control theories. *American Sociological Review, 52*, 826 – 840.

Mayer, G.R. (1995). Preventing anti-social behavior in the schools. Journal of Applied Behavioral Analysis, 467-478.

McLaughlin, C.S. (1987). *Parent-teacher conferencing.* Springfield, IL: Charles C. Thomas.

Miller, J.M. (1998). When parents meet: Teacher teams. *The Education Digest, 64*(4), 65-66.

Mills, D., & Bulach, V. S. (1996). *Behavior disordered students in collaborative/cooperative class: Does behavior improve?* Tampa, FL: Eric Document Reproduction Service No. ED394224.

Morris, R.C. (1996). The contrasting disciplinary models in education. *Thresholds in Education, 22* (4), 7 – 13.

Mountrose, P.C. (1999). Getting through to kids 6 to 18. Education Digest, 64 (1), 10 – 17.

Naeef, R.A. (1997). Special children challenged parents: The struggles and rewards of raising a child with a disability. *Exceptional Parents, 27*, 21.

National Association for the Education of Young Children (NAEYC) and the National Association of Early Childhood Specialists in State Department of Education. (2002). *Early standards: Creating the conditions for success.* Washington, DC: NAEYC.

National Center for Educational Statistics (1999, January). *Teacher quality:* A report on the preparation and quality of public school teachers. U.S. Department of Education.

National Commission on Excellence in Education. (1982). *A nation at risk: The importance of education reform.* Washington, DC: U.S. Government Printing Office.

National State Board of Education. (1992). *Winners all: A call for inclusive schools.* Washington, DC: NASBE.

Nelsen, J., Lott, L., & Glenn, H.S. (1993). *Positive discipline in the classroom.* Rocklin, CA: Prima.

Nelson, J.R., Crabtree, M. Marchand, Martella, N., & Martell, R. (1998). Teaching good behavior in the whole school. *Teaching exceptional children, 30* (4), 4-9.

Nodding, N. (1982). *The challenge to care in school: An alternative approach to education.* New York: Teacher College Press.

Oakes, J., & Lipton, M. (1999). *Teaching to change the world.* Boston: McGraw-Hill.

O'Brien, J., & O'Brien, C. (1991). *Members of each: Perspectives of social support for people with severe disabilities.* Lithuania, GA: Responsive Systems Associates.

Ogbu, J. (1988). Class stratification, racial stratification, and schooling. In L. Weis (Ed.), *Class, Race, and Gender in American Education.* Albany, NY: State University of New York Press.

Ohlrich, K.B. (1996). Parent volunteers: An asset to your technology plan. *Learning and Leading with Technology, 24,* 51-52.

Okagaki, L., & French, P.A. (1998). Parenting and children's school achievement: A multiethnic perspective. *American Educational Research Journal, 25,*123-144.

Payne, R. (1998). *A framework for understanding poverty.* Baytown, TX: RFT Publishing.

Pennsylvania Department of Education, Bureau of Special Education. (1995). Guidelines: *Effective behavioral support.* Harrisonburg, PA: Author.

Poplin, M.S. (1988). Holistic/constructivist principles of the teaching/learning process : Implications for the field of learning disabilities. *Journal of Learning Disabilities, 21,* 410 – 416.

Potter, L. (1996). Making school parent-friendly. *Education Digest, 62,* 28-30.

Powell, D.R., (1998). Re-weaving parents into early childhood education programs. *Education Digest, 64* (3), 22-25.

Solo, L. (1997). School success begins at home. *Principal, 77* (2), 29-30.

Reavis, H.K., Kukic, S.J., Jenson, W.R., Morgan, D.P., Andrews, D.J., & Fister, S.,(1996). *Best practices.* Longmont, CO: Sopris West Publishers.

Research Connections in Special Education. (1997). ERIC/OSEP Special Project. *The Eric Clearinghouse on Disabilities and Gifted Education, 1* (1), 1-8.

Resnick, M.D., Bearman, P. Blum, R., Bauman, K., Harris, K., Jones, J., Tabor, J., Beuhring, T., Sieving, R., Shew, M., Ireland, M., Bearinger, L., & Udry, J. (1997). Protecting adolescents from harm-Findings from the national longitudinal study on adolescent health. *Journal of the American Medical Association, 278,*(10), 823–832.

Rhode, G., Jenson, W.R., & Reavis, H.K. (1992). *The tough kid book: Practical classroom management strategies.* Longmont, CO: Sopris West.

Rizzo, J.V., & Zabel, R.H. (1988). *Educating children and adolescents with behavioral disorders: An integrative approach.* Boston: Allyn and Bacon, Inc.

Rogers, C.R. (1969). *Freedom to learn.* Englewood Cliffs, NJ: Prentice Hall.

Santin, J. (1998). Longer school days on the way? *Herald Journal, 89* (140), 1ff.

Santrock, J.W. (1976). Affect and facilitative self-control. Influence of ecological setting, cognition, and social agent. *Journal of Educational Psychology, 68* (5), 529–535.

Sapphire, P. (1999). Know all your students to reduce violence. *The Education Digest, 65* (1), 4 – 5.

Savage, T.V. (1991). *Discipline for self-control.* Englewood Cliffs, NJ: Prentice-Hall.

Seiler, W.J., Schuelke, L.D., & Lieb-Brilhart, B.(1984). *Communication for the contemporary classroom.* New York: Holt, Reinhart, & Wilson.

Shearer, J. (1988). Foul language: Classroom trouble. In J.H. Shulman and J.A. Colbert (Eds.). *The intern teacher case book.* Eugene, OR: ERIC Clearing House on Education..

Slavin, R. (1995). *Cooperative learning* (2nd ed.). Boston: Allyn & Bacon.

Steinberg, L. (1996). *Beyond the classroom: Why school reform has failed and what parents need to do.* New York: Simon & Schuster.

Steward, C. (1996). The coach-parent meeting: The initial contact. *Strategies, 10,* 13-15.

Straus, M., Gelles, R. and Steinmetz, S. (1980). *Behind closed doors: Violence in the American Family.* New York. Anchor Press/Doubleday.

Stuart, R.B. (1989). Social learning theory: A vanishing or expanding presence? *Psychology: A Journal of Human Behavior, 26,* 135 – 150.

Suqai, G., & Pruitt, R. (1993). *Phases, steps, and guidelines for building school-wide behavior management programs: A practitioner's handbook.* Oregon: Behavior Disorders Program.

Swick, K. L., & Broadway, F. (1997). Parental efficacy and successful parent involvement. *Journal of Instructional Psychology, 24,* 69-75.

Taylor, G.R. (1992). Impact of social learning on educating deprived/minority children. *Clearinghouse for Teacher Education.* (ERIC Document Reproduction Service No. Ed. 349260).

Taylor, G.R. (1992). Integrating social learning theory in educating the deprived. ED. *Clearinghouse for Education.* ERIC 349260.

Taylor, G.R. (1997). *Curriculum strategies: Social skills interventions for young African-American males.* Westport, CT: Praeger Press.

Taylor, G.R. (1998). *Curriculum strategies for teaching social skills to the disabled: Dealing with inappropriate behaviors.* Springfield, IL. Charles C. Thomas.

Taylor, G.R. (1999). *Curriculum models and strategies for educating individuals with disabilities in inclusive classrooms.* Springfield, IL: Charles C. Thomas.

Taylor, G.R. (2000). *Parental involvement: A practical guide for collaboration and teamwork for students with disabilities.* Springfield, IL. Charles C. Thomas.

Taylor, G. R. (2001). *Educational intervention and services for children with exceptionalities.* Springfield, IL: Charles C Thomas.

The National Association of State Boards of Education (1992). Alexandria, VA, p. 13.

Tharp, R.G. (1989). Psychocultural variables and constraints: Effects on teaching and learning in schools. *American Psychologists, 44*, 349 – 359.

Thomas, A., & Grimes, J. (1995). *Best practices in school psychology III*, Silver Spring, MD: National Association of School Psychologists.

Thompson, J.C., & Walter, J.K. (1999). School disciplines becoming proactice, productive, participatory, and predictable. *Annual Editions, Education*, 99-100.

Thompson, S. (1998). Moving from publicity to engagement. *Educational Leadership, 55*(8), 54-57.

Trent, S.C., Driver, B.L., Wood, M.H., Parrott, P.S., Martin, T.F., & Smith, W.G. (1995). *Creating and sustaining a special education/general education partnership: A story of evolution, change, and uncertainty.* Unpublished manuscript, Michigan State University.

Turnbull, H.R., & Turnbull, A.P. (1998). *Free appropriate public education* (5th ed.). Denver: Love Publishing.

Utley, C.A., Mortweet, S.L. & Greenwood, C.P., (1997). Peer-mediated instruction and intervention. *Focus on Exceptional Children*, 29 (5), 1-23.

Van Horn, K.L. (1982). *The Utah pupil teacher self-concept program: Teacher strategies that invite improvement of pupil and teacher self-concepts.* New York: A paper presented at the annual meeting of the American Education Research Association.

Varner, E. (1999). Making discipline problems improve instruction. *The Education Digest, 65* (1), 18 – 20.

Veenman, S. (1998). Cognitive and non-cognitive effects of multi-grade and multi-age classes: A best-evidence synthesis. *Review of Educational Research, 65* (4), 319–381.

Vincent, J. P. (1990). *The biology of emotions.* Cambridge, MA: Basil Blackwell.

Wang, J., Wildman, L., & Calhound, G. (1996). The relationship between parental influences and student achievement in seventh grade mathematics. *School Science and Mathematics, 96,* 395-399.

Wang, M.C., Haertel, G.D., & Walberg, H.J. (1993). Toward a knowledge base for school learning. *Review of Educational Research, 63*(3), 249-294.

Wang, M. C., Haertel, G. D., & Walberg, H. J. (1994). What helps students learn? *Educational Leadership, 51* (4), 74–79.

Walker, H.M. (1995). *The acting out child. Coping with classroom disruption* (2nd ed.). Longmont, CO: Sopris West.

Walker, H. M., Colvin, G., & Ramsey, E., (1995). *Antisocial behavior in school: Strategies and best practices.* Pacific Grove, CA: Brooks/Cole.

Walker, H.M. (1997). *First step: An early intervention program for anti-social kindergartners.* Reston, VA: *The Council for Exceptional Children.*

Walker, H. M., Horner, R., Suqai, G. Bullis, M., Sprague, J., Bricker, D., & Kaufman, M. (1996). Integrated approaches to preventing anti-social behavior patterns among school-age children and youth. *Journal of Emotional and Behavioral Disorders, 4,* 193-256.

White, A.E., & White, L.L. (1992). A collaborative model for students with mild disabilities in middle schools. *Focus on Exceptional Children, 24*(9), 1-10.

Whiteford, T. (1998). Math for moms and dads. *Educational Leadership, 55*(8), 64-66.

Wilson, J.H. (1997). Communication, collaboration, caring family, center care. *Exceptional Parent,* 28, 61.

Wolf, J.M. (1998). Just read. *Educational Leadership, 55*(8), 61-63.

Woolfolk, A.E. (1993). *Educational psychology* (5th ed). Boston: Allyn & Bacon.

Zlatos, C. (1994). Teaching discipline and classroom management: An annotated guide through the literature. *Teacher Education,* 6 (1), 167-178.

About The Author

George R. Taylor, Ph.D. is Professor of Special Education and Chairperson Emeritus of the Department of Special Education at Coppin State College, and CORE Faculty, The Union Institute and University. His knowledge and expertise in the areas of Research and Special Education are both locally and nationally renown. He has made significant contributions through Research and Publications in the areas of Special Education, Research, and Education. Additionally, Dr. Taylor has directed several large Federal Research grants and conducted numerous workshops and seminars throughout the country.

Lois Nixon, Ph.D. is Professor of Special Education at Coppin State College, where she is also the Coordinator of the Undergraduate Special Education Program. She is responsible for the development and evolution of the program and has had extensive experiences working with individuals with special needs. Dr. Nixon has contributed to the professional literature in Special Education through publications and curriculum development.

George R. Taylor, Ph.D is professor of Special Education and Chair Emeritus, Department of Special Education at Coppin State College, Baltimore Maryland, and Core Faculty, the Union Institute and University, Cincinnati, Ohio. His knowledge and expertise in education is both locally and nationally renown. He has made significant contributions through research and publications in the fields of Special Education and Research Methods. He has published nine textbooks and over 20 professional articles. Additionally, Dr. Taylor has directed several federal grants and conducted numerous workshops and seminars for teachers at the local, state, and national levels.

Lois Nixon, Ph.D is professor of Special Education at Coppin State College, where she is also the Coordinator of the Undergraduate Special Education Program. She is responsible for the development and evolution of the program and has had extensive experiences working with individuals with special needs. Dr. Nixon has contributed to the professional literature in Special Education through publications and curriculum development.

188 Index